From *the* Ground Up

A Lifelong

Journey

in Reinventing

Yourself

From *the* Ground Up

A Lifelong Journey in Reinventing Yourself

The Biography of BRIAN PECON
by DAVID YAWN *and* DARRELL USELTON

CORPORATE CHRONICLES
A Lighthouse Leadership Imprint
David Yawn Communications

First American Edition
ISBN 978-0-615-35905-2

＊

Corporate Chronicles
A Lighthouse Memoirs Imprint
David Yawn Communications
1082 Kings Park Road
Memphis 38117

＊

Designed by BrianGroppe Design

CONTENTS

To each member of my immediate family, especially my daughters Pamela, Priscilla and Trish who have withstood their father's journey gyrations during more than forty years of my ever-changing career reinventions. Fortunately, their levels of good-natured tolerance have been passed along to my seven grandchildren who will hopefully persevere through their own lives in an unknown future America. Unfortunately, my devoted spouse of over 48 years, Peg, was not able to witness the product of this final manuscript, but it was her efforts that kept our family together as one unit and built the basic foundation of trust and faith that allowed our family to flourish.

Our church family as a faith community, additionally, proved to be a source of learning, edification and fellowship.

Lastly, to my father and mother who instilled the family, work and faith values of America's 1940s and 1950s, enabling our American dream to be fulfilled and to be able to live my journey from the ground up.

If you have made mistakes,

even serious ones, there is always

another chance for you. What we call

failure is not the falling down,

but the staying down.

—MARY PICKFORD

INTRODUCTION

According to some, Brian E. Pecon would seem on the surface to be much like any professional. He is successful by all economic measures, but works and deeds are much harder to judge. By definition, success can be difficult to gauge because it means different things to different people. To Brian Pecon, success ultimately encompasses not only what is obtained by material gain through professional pursuits, but also holistically, from spiritual, family and other aspects of one's life.

As his story unfolds, one undoubtedly will witness a unique man who regularly employed critical leadership and decision-making skills in his unrelenting drive to succeed. These skills have given him a measure of personal and professional achievement, at the same time allowing him to discover his true purpose in life.

For most of us, moments of inspiration and accomplishment often are followed by periods of frustration and dread. Unlike many, Brian has displayed remarkable tenacity for perseverance at such times. When faced with tough management decisions, he is guided by both inspiration and a commitment to "do the right thing" – a character attribute rarely seen in today's society and business world.

Brian's life has been dynamic and one actively dedicated to military, business, government and community arenas. Significant milestones of his career include his service with the Strategic Air Command, American Airlines, FedEx, an international business life, a local city/county economic development office, the Episcopal Church and other occupational venues that are highlighted throughout this book. His life's work and decision-making purviews together create an irresistible and unique story for those interested in how decisions – both personal and corporate – are crafted in an increasingly fast-paced and complex world. These chapters display true-life lessons in how one person can make a difference.

If one were to select just a few hallmarks of his life work, then vision, perspective and persistence would be among the main elements. These traits evolved primarily from his relationship with his father, honed from the experiences he faced as a youngster growing up in Western Massachusetts and from the challenges and opportunities he encountered throughout his life. In retrospect, Brian's numerous challenges became his competitive advantage. He developed a penchant for quickly analyzing key issues and developing solutions. Often, he made sidesteps in his decision-making, but in the long run, the problems were methodically and effectively solved to his satisfaction. As a business leader, he regularly displayed the ability to make critical decisions on both small and large scales after assembling the available facts and contingencies. As the reader will learn, even his misjudgments carry instructive value.

As Brian reflects on his life, he has a compelling story to tell. As he navigated through various stages of his professional life, the path held challenges, upsets and victories. In the midst of it all, Brian tenaciously steered a straight course, unwilling to yield to momentary discouragement. He adapted, he remained flexible and he persevered, emerging intact and as a much wiser man.

1

New England Childhood Experience

(1940s, 1950s)

Brian Pecon was born in Great Barrington, Massachusetts, a small New England town of 5,500 on February 8, 1937, during a time when two world leaders dominated the headlines. FDR was trying to lead America out of the Great Depression, while half a globe away, Adolph Hitler was building a war machine in hopes of conquering the world.

Unlike many people struck by these hard times, Brian's early years were relatively free from need. His father, Leon, worked as a trucking company manager and his mother, Diana, kept the household running, along with his maternal Scots-born grandmother, Elizabeth Rankin. Over time and through personal observation, he acquired a strong work ethic from his father and mother and learned early on to be independent and a self-starter.

As World War II was winding down across the Atlantic and Pacific oceans, the hardworking Pecon family was busy going through the day-in, day-out activities of school, work and church. Young Brian didn't have much time to play kickball in the neighborhood lot. He was getting his first lessons in persistence and perseverance in this New England Berkshire County mill town. The fact that he could juggle the responsibilities of a job and school would be a novelty today, but became the norm for him.

ALL WORK AND LITTLE PLAY

Brian's father, Leon, was born in 1907 and grew up with the rigid hardworking farm mentality. He came from a large family with three brothers and three sisters. With his French Huguenot background, he was an independent, self-made and responsible father and husband. Brian's mother, Diana, was a

February 1944, Brian at age 7.

first-generation American from a Scottish background, with only one brother. Neither of his parents had a college education, so they were of the mindset that their children would go out and work hard for a living. They often said to Brian, "If you want a car when you're older, you're going to have to pay for it yourself."

Leon was a hard-driving man and eventually served as a mentor for Brian's strong work ethic. Brian had many mentors through the years, such as Harland B. Foster, a friend of the family and business owner for whom he later worked during the summers of his college years both as a steamfitter's assistant and as an electrician's assistant.

In the middle 1950s, jobs were very hard to come by for young people, especially in a small town. His first paying job was mowing lawns at the age of 10. By age 12, he added an early morning newspaper route to his routine prior to going to school, and at age 14, Brian was stocking shelves at a local drug store in his hometown. "I worked there six days a week and can still tell you all the pharmaceutical brands and alcoholic beverages in the store."

The majority of the residents in Great Barrington were Catholic. Being Protestant gave him an interesting distinction. If you were a young boy playing on a baseball team during this time, there was a good chance there would be one or two Protestants to eight or nine Catholic teammates. However, being in the religious minority was never a problem for him.

A "NORMAN ROCKWELL" LIFE

Much of the excitement in the town was seasonal, and still is, in this Berkshire County old resort atmosphere where the population doubles in the summertime and tourists fly or drive up from New York to see the changing autumn foliage in the fall. Visitors and tourists from the greater New York

Brian's boyhood home in Great Barrington, MA.

City area have chosen Great Barrington over the years for cozy, yet increasingly expensive, vacation retreat homes. The flip side is that the resort area also feels the brunt of New England winters the rest of the year.

Delivering daily newspapers, such as *The New York Times*, in frigid and snowy mornings was a character and stamina-builder. However, bicycles don't work well in the wintertime on frozen snow. Brian later recalled, "One of the biggest reasons I did not want to stay in New England was the weather. The winters are fun when you're a kid, but when you're older, you have to do a lot of shoveling. From late September to April it is mostly gloom and doom up there. It just hangs over you and affects your outlook. It can be very depressing. I knew I did not want to live in a small town, so I couldn't wait to discover the greater world after high school. It's funny thinking about it now, with out-of-state residents flocking there all year long."

EARLY PASSIONS

Sometime around the age of 12, he began an early avocation that would lead to a larger career down the road. Brian started building model airplanes – the old way out of balsa wood and tissue paper. This was in a day preceding

Christmas 1947. Left to right; siblings Janice and Bruce with Brian.

plastic model kits with instruction sheets and circled parts numbers. It was a precursor to his growing interest in aviation as a vocation – a dream that would later become a reality.

Brian also had a love for cars. When he turned 16 in 1953, Brian had saved enough money to buy his first car, a goal for which most young men strive. With this achievement, he learned one of his most important lessons as a young man – success comes from hard work. He purchased a 1940 Chevrolet sedan with a standard shift that he was able to park in the family garage, a barn-looking structure on the property that was built in the early 1900s. The barn helped minimize the winter snow accumulation during the frequent snow showers that could last into April. As an impetuous teenager, he collaborated one Sunday night with a school friend during a period of boredom to test drive his new car, which had not yet been registered. Learning the art of risk-taking at an early age, Brian recalls fabricating a fake license plate of white cardboard for the rear license holder. This ingenious idea created the image of a properly registered vehicle and allowed him to drive his car against his father's wishes.

The family lived in a hilly section of town and Brian and his friend began tooling around in the newly bought Chevy, going up and down a few hills and finally coming down one near the local New York, New Haven & Hartford Railroad passenger station. Suddenly, the brakes began to fail as they began to descend the steep slope. Faced with a quick decision, Brian had to decide to stay with the car or jump out onto the hard concrete pavement, leaving the car to careen dangerously down the hill. With the brakes gone and gaining speed, he continued to pump the brake pedal, but to no avail. He engaged and re-engaged the clutch, which made matters worse, and the emergency brake was of no help. Suddenly, they both realized the car was out of control. At this point, his friend decided to bail out while the bailing was good. Maybe it was his growing maturity coupled with a sense of responsibility and a willingness to see things through that compelled him to stay at the wheel, but Brian decided to ride it out. Finally, the car inauspiciously met a cement pole and came to a sudden stop with its front end two feet above the ground and resting between two parked cars. Both of the mischievous boys were fortunate as neither of them were seriously injured.

Eventually, the local police arrived at the scene and the embarrassing make-shift license was quickly discovered and found to belong to another vehicle in Brockton, Massachusetts, some 25 miles south of Boston. Brian's driver's license was quickly pocketed by the local chief of police for the next 30 days, a fairly light punishment by today's standards, while the "hot rod" was repaired. Not surprisingly, the car was kept in the family garage during the entire license suspension. As one would suspect, his father was less than supportive of his son's risk-taking venture as a strict curfew was imposed during the suspension period. Even though he didn't realize the life-lesson at the time, he did sense the need for a purpose in life and for setting a goal of making something of himself. Remarkably, this lesson left him with a sense of adventure for the sake of excitement. In other words, the experience didn't inhibit him from taking risks that might result in failure.

DREAMS OF ADVENTURE

One such risk was leaving the security of home and family for pursuits in unknown territory. His growing sense of adventure didn't seem to fit a life in Great Barrington. Brian had been thinking of breaking loose and getting away from his boyhood home after his high school graduation. With a graduating class of only 53, there was the sense that everything you did was seen by a condensed huddle of hometown citizenry. In his mind, home was beginning to be a microcosm where everyone was aware of your every move.

It's all wrapped up in a kind of innate pride of independence in the hearts of true New Englanders, whether they are considered either landside or boaters. There were always aspirations percolating in Brian's mind that extended beyond normal teenage interests in sports, cars and girls. This high school student knew that if he buckled down and thought seriously about the course of his work, he'd eventually get somewhere. Maybe he would become a pilot someday, but that would take a lot of study and hard work academically. He wasn't particularly enthralled with doing homework, but in his junior year he started to pursue math and other college entry-level type courses with higher goals in mind. He was quoted as saying, "Because I was not the smartest guy on the block, I knew I would need to really push hard academically to succeed in whatever I chose to do." Even as a teenager, Brian was thinking about a life in aviation. He would often visit the small airport just outside of Great Barrington operated by Walt Koladza. Walt was the original long-time proprietor of the airport for over 50 years and only recently passed away. Many years later Brian thought about purchasing the grass strip airfield, although he never pursued the idea further.

Brian's relationship with his father, Leon, contributed enormously to his personality and drive during his early years. Unfortunately, their relationship was not a positive one. According to Brian, his father was very dictatorial and they always seemed at odds when he was growing up. "I held a lot against him for a long time. We were very much alike – two strong-willed people always going at each other." This confrontation concerned his mother for years, always wishing they could have had a less hostile relationship. "We never had father and son talks or confided in one another. He and I weren't built like that. He rarely asked me about my future plans, because he was always too busy with his own business. As I reflect on my father now, that is probably where I get a lot of my drive and ambition, but it also contributed to my leaving home to strike out on my own." Sadly, Brian and his father never experienced a close relationship until near the end of his father's life.

It was many years later that Brian realized that his father had always been a mentor to him, setting the example for hard work and perseverance. "But when you're working and raising a family, you don't have much time to think about those things. I wouldn't have said this a few years ago, but now at 73, I remember comparing myself to what he did. My father was a self-made guy who considered his work, family and religion very important. That was always a core foundation of what he did." Upon reflection, Brian understood late in life that his father's influence and mentorship had always been there, though he was not consciously aware of it. His mother, always the peacemaker, played a somewhat neutral role, but always dedicated herself to keeping peace in the family.

BRIAN'S LESSONS LEARNED:

1. Know your limitations, but don't be afraid of taking risks.

2. Make your own decisions and be prepared for the outcomes.

3. Understand the value of persistence and hard work.

2

COLLEGE DAYS AND A GLIMPSE OF THE FUTURE

(1954-1957)

Aviation was Brian's first passion in life. He dreamed of someday becoming an Air Force pilot, but knew it would require a personal commitment and a lot of self-discipline to reach this lofty goal. At the same time, Brian never considered academics as one of his chief strengths. In order to succeed in aviation, he would have to have a serious academic plan and stick with it. With this in mind, he strategically chose the technical route to overcome the challenges that awaited him. He decided to pursue an A&P (FAA approved) Class A mechanic's license, a course of study which offered technical as well as aviation courses that would bring him one step closer to his goal.

CONVENTIONAL COLLEGE LIFE

After considering several colleges, he chose Boston University's College of Industrial Technology (CIT) because it offered an aviation component that was central to his plan. Granted, there were other schools, such as two-year junior colleges, but they didn't hold the same aviation allure. While most college kids at the time were motivated and focused on a conventional four-year college curriculum, Brian believed the technical college route would prove the best course of action. "Four years of college was not for me then, as my future hinged on getting into the USAF pilot training program." His approach worked as he enjoyed repairing objects of all kinds, and was used to the systems-type approach to solving problems. The decision to take the

Boston University College of Engineering.

technical courses ultimately proved to be the right course of action and created many opportunities that would not have been possible had he chosen another route.

He entered Boston University in the fall of 1954 at age 17 with the goal of obtaining his air frame and power plant license. This move would prove to be valuable to Brian for all aspects of aircraft maintenance. After about a year at BU, he built up some contacts and gained a major interest in what was then the Aviation Cadet Program with the U.S. Air Force. This was three years before the Air Force Academy was in place at Colorado Springs. Jet aircraft were still a somewhat new and developing technology in the late 1950s, having debuted in force a few years earlier in the Korean War. One could still see a predominance of prop aircraft on military and civilian tarmacs during that time period.

Brian's college life was somewhat conventional. He lived in the primary men's dorm, Myles Standish Hall, during his first year. In his second year he moved to a small two-room apartment in the Fensgate area, within sight of Fenway Park. While many of the students commuted to Boston University, Brian was forced to live on campus since the college was 150 miles from his hometown of Great Barrington. He was a serious student and concentrated on his dream of flying Air Force jets. He chose not to join a fraternity and spent little time getting into the campus scene.

Brian had three roommates: Michael Lipstein, a Jewish Brooklynite majoring in business, Charles Auburn, a Catholic performing arts major from Stamford, Conn., and Jim Aseltine, a Protestant liberal arts major from rural Enosburg Falls, Vt. He got along best with Jim and they roomed together the following two years. To help with school expenses, Brian parked cars in public parking lots on weekends and weekdays at both Bruins and Celtics games plus other popular area sports engagements at the Boston Garden and the Boston Arena. "It was an easy way to make quick dollars without training or experience, and you quickly learned the ways of the streets as well as the MTA subway system. This was before I had my own car in Boston."

Cars were parked with the keys still in the ignitions during the events to allow cars to be maneuvered closer together later to accommodate more autos. During very busy games, they would have to park the cars on the street and were often queried by a surly policeman about why cars were parked on public streets. The obvious reply was that they had run out of lot space. Often, such actions were reported but rarely led to personal discipline. Later, it was learned that regular payoff schemes were common.

THE SUMMER OF '56

There were other jobs that taught Brian the value of a day's work and a day's pay. One summer stands out when he sold his 1940 Chevy and bought a 1950 Ford for $300. His roommate, Jim Aseltine, had an aunt and uncle in Pomona, California so Brian and Jim decided to venture traveling there to work during the summer of 1956. With Aseltine paying for the oil and gas, the two teenagers set out. The cost of oil was important because Brian's Ford used a quart every 300 miles. The tires were also a concern but they fortunately held up for the duration of the trip. "That was a maturing point for me," he said. The one-week journey to California, sleeping in the car at night, included traveling along the famed Route 66, stopping in Las Vegas along the way, and being rejected at the casino doors for being underage. Upon their arrival in California, they stayed several weeks with Jim's aunt and uncle. The remainder of their time was spent with the boys at the University of Southern California's Delta Chi fraternity house through a connection from Jim's uncle. Before moving in the house, they spent several nights at the local YMCA which, according to Brian, was a poor decision. "The car was broken into on the first night, but they only took Jim's clothes. The LA police took fingerprints from the car but we never heard back from them."

Their first job in California was selling encyclopedias on commission door to door near Long Beach. "It was the only commission job I ever took, and it convinced me it was not a long term endeavor." Later, both got jobs with steady paychecks at Bullocks Department Store in downtown Los Angeles, where they worked the whole course of the summer making about $50 a week. Brian recalled, "The pay wasn't all that great, but it was definitely a good location to meet the opposite sex." Much of their off duty time was spent cruising the beaches and sightseeing in Beverly Hills.

In the meantime, the two dealt with new environments and several new experiences: the California style of living and liberal values, something rarely seen in rural New England, and the smog. This broadening of Brian's horizons convinced him of several things. One was sensory; the climate was great, but California's smog and pollution controls were not as stringent as they are today. Fortunately, he worked inside at Bullocks, but still suffered for three months with watery eyes and breathing issues. Another enlightening episode was somewhat amusing. While driving to work one summer morning on the unpredictable Santa Monica Freeway, they ran out of gas and had to coast down a hill at the exit to a nearby gas station. With payday still a few days away, they only had enough money for three or four gallons of gas. Nevertheless, it was enough to keep the car going, but they learned to keep a sharper eye on the gas gauge.

Other experiences were longer lasting. Brian learned to be independent and live on his own; secondly, he realized he wanted to move ahead in his education. He also discovered that stocking shelves in the house wares department was not his life-long pursuit. All in all, the experience allowed the 19 year-old an opportunity in risk-taking – to venture out on his own and learn to be resourceful. He vividly remembered the day he and Jim left California's San Fernando Valley and entered the countryside on their return trip to New England. He was physically relieved as he breathed fresh air once again and said goodbye to skies filled with leaded auto exhaust. The return trip was much more pleasurable as it took them through the beautiful Yellowstone National Park and the Black Hills of South Dakota - again sleeping in the car each night.

BECOMING AN AIR FORCE CADET

Brian received an Associate in Science degree from Boston University in January of 1957 after two and a half challenging years of technical training. While most of his classmates continued with aviation maintenance careers, Brian voluntarily took the USAF aviation cadet entry exams at Westover Air Force Base in Springfield, Mass. To gain a class entry date, there were several factors that converged to his benefit with uncanny timing. The aviation cadet

Red's Riders – (L to R) Cadet Brian Pecon, Red Gargaly,
2nd Lt. Charles Mead, Cadet Roger Kobylak, Moultrie, GA, 1958.

program would allow a non-four year degree student to receive an officer's commission and a pilot's rating without a bachelor's degree. This was a program emanating from the time of World War II, allowing more eligible pilot candidates when there was a shortage of four-year officers. It was part of his strategy. "I was trying to squeeze in under that interim program," he recalls. It was a fast-track 15-month curriculum, albeit under vigorous requirements.

He took the entrance exam and was surprised by the complexity of some of the questions but, fortunately, took a straightforward approach with his answers and passed. The courses he took during his junior and senior years in high school began to pay off. His knowledge of science, math and physics certainly helped, as did his ability to conceptualize – a trait that would help him later in life. What is remarkable is that he had never flown in an airplane at that point – even as a passenger, much less as a pilot.

Knowing the mechanical elements of how a plane could fly basically got him by. He had picked that up in technical courses at BU. He knew how ailerons, for instance, would alter a plane's course in the sky and how instrumentation worked – at least conceptually. "Some candidates tried to second guess the USAF entrance exam questions and that got them into trouble. I just took the logical approach, not viewing each question as a trick question. It worked." It also got him to the next stage.

This was also the time in which Brian met his future wife, Margaret (Peg) Ann Beattie, a Scots-Irish young lady from a large Catholic family of four brothers and four sisters. She lived in Pittsfield, Mass., only 20 miles from his hometown of Great Barrington, and had graduated from high school in the same year as Brian, 1954. The initial meeting occurred just after Jim and Brian returned from their California trip and directly prior to his returning to BU for the fall semester. It was a 1956 Labor Day picnic at Lake Buel near Great Barrington. The party was given by Peg's employer – First Agricultural Bank of Berkshire County. One might visualize a scene out of the musical, "Picnic." Brian remembered vividly, "Two friends of mine, Danny Broderick and Norman Roux, met three girls from the bank at the party. Each of us quickly paired up with one of the girls and, subsequently, had dates for a week or so before we went back to our respective schools." Brian and Peg kept in contact through periodic letter exchanges until he returned from BU in late January, 1957 prior to his acceptance to the Air Force Cadet program in May of that year.

After the aviation cadet tests, Brian didn't hear from the Air Force for months. Not receiving an acceptance letter to the program after such a long period of time caused him to believe there was a problem. Did he actually make the grade? Was he mistaken about his standing? As luck would have it, he received an acceptance letter in the mail, but not from the Air Force. The U.S. Navy offered him a chance to enter their aviation cadet program. Without an official "go" from the Air Force, he briefly considered a career in the Navy aircraft carrier program as an option. However, he decided to wait for his chances with the USAF. In this era of the mandatory military draft he had several choices. He could have elected to go into a four-year officer program as an enlisted person, take his chances with the draft under a college deferment, or wait for his cadet examination results. A month later, he received the long awaited good news that he had been accepted in the Air Force Cadet Program. In retrospect, it was somewhat remarkable because during the Cold War era there was a low pilot demand and military instructors looked for ways to "wash out" cadets once they were admitted, through military, ground school or flying performance.

With test results back, he was assigned to Class 59B with an entry date of May 22, 1957, a date he still readily recalls. He was very curious about what was ahead as he anticipated the cadet program that would ultimately last one year, three months and 12 days. He subsequently counted down each one of these days until the commission graduation date. No one in his immediate family had previously served in the military. It was only due to family size (three sons and a daughter) that his father was not drafted into the Navy near the end of World War II. Additionally, his experiential knowledge of flying was zero, so he knew he was in for an eye-opener. "I was determined to survive and thrive in a world where no one else in the immediate family had ventured."

BRIAN'S LESSONS LEARNED:

1. Pursue the dreams you are passionate about.

2. Broaden your horizons by being independent and resourceful.

3

MILITARY EXPERIENCE

(1957-1958)

During the late 1950s and early 1960s, the United States found itself in the midst of a very real Cold War period, even though it was a few steps removed from a hot war. It also coincided with the jump start to the Space Age. The Korean War was over and in 1959 the Air Force Academy graduated its first class at Colorado Springs, Colo. The Titan, Atlas and Minuteman missiles were in development and so was the legendary X-15.

In the space program, America's second Project Mercury astronaut, Capt. Virgil I. Grissom, attained an altitude of 118 miles and flew 5,310 mph in a 303-mile sub-orbital space flight from Cape Canaveral in the Liberty Bell 7 capsule. Maj. Robert M. White attained a top speed of 4,093 mph in an X-15 hypersonic rocket plane while flying at full throttle at an altitude of 101,600 feet.

FIRST FLIGHT INTO THE CADET PROGRAM

May 22, 1957 was a very important date that started a new phase of Brian's life. It began with Peg driving him to be sworn in at Springfield, Conn. She bid him farewell at Bradley Field, the airport serving both Springfield and Hartford. He boarded the TWA Lockheed Constellation flight to San Antonio with much anticipation and excitement. It was significant because it represented his first-ever commercial flight. The flight seemed rather uneventful because things were happening so fast. When he arrived at Lackland Air Force Base, which was the primary airman and cadet-training base in the USA, he found himself in the heat of this post-Korean Cold War period and also that of the steaming Texas summer sun.

"The whole thing went by so fast that I never gave it much thought. I didn't realize what I was stepping into." He didn't have family or friends to brief him on what to expect upon his arrival regarding what military cadet life was like. Again, Brian's level-headed strategy was applied. Just do what the instructors and upper classmen tell you to do and don't take it personally – no matter how or what they ordered.

The training that awaited him had three distinct phases. The first was a 12-week preflight ground phase, followed by a 6-month primary stage where he would learn elementary flying, and lastly, the basic flight training phase in either a single-engine jet or a multi-engine reciprocating aircraft. In total, it amounted to a year, three months and 12 days – a time period he would never forget. The first two weeks of preflight training was difficult for Brian to absorb and he counted down every day during the training. The preflight training phase was also one of the most emotional periods of Brian's life. "For six weeks, you're an underclassman and then for six weeks, you're an upper-classman. Our class size was about 100 cadets with every type of background imaginable, ranging in age from 19 and a half to 26," Brian recalls. To be in that group, a cadet had to be between the heights of 5'-4" to 6'-4." If they were bigger or smaller, they didn't qualify. Restrictions were tighter during this time period because there was not a demand for pilots and females were not yet accepted into the program.

There was a real combination of trainees coming in with varied backgrounds. Some candidates came from various state Air National Guard units, some were regular Air Force enlisted people with aviation backgrounds and some were civilians. The National Guard folks knew they would be flying specific types of jets stateside after they finished. For instance, Ronald Jacobsen (Jake), his roommate from Stafford Springs, Conn., was in the Connecticut Air National Guard and would ultimately fly F-86s.

"WASH OUTS"

"There wasn't a great demand for incoming pilots at that time. For instance, if you didn't have good teeth, you could be washed out, even after grueling initial flight physicals. There was also the requirement to stand at attention while in formation in that hot San Antonio summer sun. If you passed out or fainted and your knees touched the ground, you were gone." If you didn't wash out, your options were limited, such as becoming an enlisted basic Airman or entering the Air Force navigator training program. There was also the option of returning home as a civilian and taking your chances with the military draft, which usually meant the U.S. Army.

After just completing two and a half years of college, the coursework was not too difficult for Brian, but the military applications were challenging. Indeed, the hardest part for him was learning military bearing. The flight portion and ground school components did not compare to the physical and psychological stress he would encounter. The cadets who had the hardest times were those who were not in good physical shape. During that first six weeks, cadets couldn't get in a car or go off base. It was a bare basic living experience. At 5:30 in the morning they would start the day with physical training by running around the athletic field, shower, get into dress uniform for breakfast, attend classes and endure more physical training in the afternoon. In between, they would have to play mind games. "Frankly, I was so uptight during the first two weeks that I didn't give much thought to Peg or my parents back home, which was probably the intent of the program." Eventually, Brian and Peg would routinely correspond while he was in training. "Peg wrote often and I did live for her letters from home. I always checked to make sure she put the stamps on upside down – our message to each other that we were still in love." To this day, I consider this period of my young life the most difficult part of my life, even tougher than the discipline my father doled out to me at home."

One day between the second and third week, Brian was placed in a confrontational situation with "Jake," his stout, fun-loving and somewhat overweight roommate from Connecticut. "We had different personalities but got along fine. Jake and I were eventually transferred to the same training base in Moultrie, Ga., but in different squadrons." There was a favorite trick among the upperclassmen to put cadets nose to nose and order them to not change their facial expressions. This could easily be accomplished during the first few weeks of training, but as the cadets began to know each other better, they learned to accept their different personalities. As time went by, maintaining a strict military decorum among the men became more difficult. When his roommate started to break his facial expression, Brian's playful side emerged and the silence was broken. Upperclassmen immediately started screaming, ultimately dispatching military demerits for menial housekeeping tasks, plus requiring the running of laps around the parade field for not controlling their emotions.

These military bearing drills again required Brian to evoke a systems approach in order to survive this type of training. He decided that as long as he didn't take the taunts and ridicule too seriously, it would be tolerable. He also focused on the fact that he only had a few more weeks before he became an upperclassman, then he would be able to reverse the roles. With this new mindset, Brian weathered the next four weeks just fine. "I began to treat the daily routine as a game, realizing it would soon be my turn at the end of the first six weeks, to turn the tables and play the upper classman role to the next class of victims. This is a game that's not going to last forever, so I learned to tolerate it."

RANK HAS ITS PRIVILEGES

Finally, after those initial six weeks, he became an upperclassman and was able to dish it out to the new underclassmen. He also received extra privileges such as going to the cadet club more often on their own schedules and even riding in a car.

"The numbers of people who washed out was about 10% in the first phase," he recalls. Since the other phases splintered off cadets into other training bases, it was hard to approximate how much attrition there was in each cadet class. The cadet training program was winding down as the Air Force Academy was ramping up. Additionally, the growing ROTC programs in colleges and universities were adding to the pilot resource pool. Brian also liked the upperclassman stage because it let him learn the ropes of leadership as well as how to assume a leadership posture.

Taking the military exams was another difficult stage of the flight training for Brian. He barely passed the two six-weeks tests and might have been washed out had it not been for the support from his TAC officer.

LEARNING TO FLY

The next stage of his training would offer another leap into the unknown, but it was one he was more than eager to take on: the flying phase. Successful pre-flight graduates were all given class assignment dates and information about when and where they were to leave for primary flight training. Classes convened primarily in Texas and the Southeast. He was assigned to Spence Air Base in Moultrie, Ga., in southern Georgia, north of Tallahassee, Fla., in the vicinity of the Okeefenokee Swamp. For the next three months, he would learn to fly the T-34, a single-engine Beechcraft. Then it was on to the more

A light-hearted Saturday morning inspection.
Spence Air Base, Moultrie, GA, 1958.

difficult and larger T-28, made by North American Aviation. Each cadet had 30 hours in the T-34 and 100 flight hours in the T-28. Most of the washouts during this period (estimated at 20 percent) were during the T-34 phase. This is the period in which a budding aviator initially determines whether and how well he can fly. To be able to fly any airplane is not that monumental, but to fly an airplane the USAF way is another matter.

The highest-ranking cadet in the primary phase came from the Air Force enlisted ranks. He previously acquired many flight hours in the back seat of a T-33 jet trainer and had considerable instrument flying experience prior to reaching the primary phase. Surprisingly, he ultimately washed out of the program due to being unable to break previous flying habits he had formed in the T-33. "That taught me the value of going into something cold and not having preconceived ideas and habits of what civilian flight instructors were looking for."

A second type of washout factor was air sickness. One of Brian's first roommates during the primary phase, a young cadet from Newark, N.J., had a terrible time. After constantly becoming nauseated, he filled his flight suit on several occasions and was ultimately assigned to navigator school in Har-lingen, Texas. "Vomiting inside the flight suit was preferable to throwing up on the instrument panel (for obvious reasons) or on the cockpit floor, because the one who vomits gets to clean up the mess. Try smelling the inside of a hot

cockpit filled with vomit." Fortunately, air sickness was not as much of an issue with Brian. He did become sick once during training after foolishly going
up for acrobatic maneuvers on an empty stomach, but quickly returned to the
ground just as fast to eat first.

"Later on in the Reserves, I often felt sick when riding in the cargo com-
partment of the C-119 and not at the controls." Low altitudes and turbulence
would often cause air sickness. Concentrating on the controls or listening to
the radio chatter often prevented air sickness for pilots because it redirected
thoughts away from the movement of the fuselage and the noise of the engines. Air sickness was obviously not as much of a factor in larger aircraft.
"The ride was relatively smooth in larger planes, plus you had box lunches and
soft drinks available, which came in handy on long flights."

"For me, the flight training was a reasonably enjoyable phase and was a
well-conducted instructional program that worked. Depending on the military needs at the time, the USAF likely ratcheted the flight training performance standards up or down."

Somewhat curiously, all of the flight instructors were civilians in the primary phase. Military bearing was not the issue to the degree it was during
the preflight phase. Since it was peace time and there was no hot war raging,
a more laid-back atmosphere existed and the cadets had the opportunity to
form a closer rapport with flight instructors.

About halfway through that segment of primary flight training, Brian experienced an interesting, albeit brief, highlight. He served as an honor guard
at Spence AFB for President Dwight Eisenhower. Standing at attention,
Brian saluted the former World War II general as he exited the Chief Executive's airplane, then called The Columbine. That was a thrill. The four-engine
Lockheed Constellation contained only a shadow of the luxuries Air Force
One has today, but was still a formidable aircraft for its time. The rest of the
flight training phase in T-28s involved the reinforcing of such techniques as
landings, takeoffs, stall recoveries, night flying and basic instrument flying.
The landing maneuvers included pitch patterns, going to a 60 degree bank
angle and pulling two or three Gs. If the Gs were too hard, the pilot could
sometimes lose consciousness. There were other dangers and occasional fatali-
ties. Flying in southern Georgia nights, it was possible for an inexperienced
pilot to get street lights confused with stars when flying at extreme bank
angles. With excessive banking, one could think one was looking at stars,

whereas they were actually ground lights. It was all part of the confusion of night flying in a rural dark countryside during initial training.

During the late 1950s, the Air Force was under contract to train South American, Middle Eastern and Southeast Asian pilots. There was also an interesting mix of American students including Annapolis and West Point graduates who chose to become Air Force officers and pilots. Aviation Cadets (without four-year degrees) were mixed with college graduates and military academy officers who also had degrees – all chasing the same USAF silver wings.

When Brian lost his New Jersey roommate to navigator training, his replacement was a pilot-candidate from Baghdad, Iraq. "Usama Ayoub Sabri was a personable fellow and to my knowledge became a good pilot. It was my first introduction into another culture and I remember how every afternoon, he set up his prayer rug with his Koran and brought out a prayer record to play in accordance with Muslim prayer tradition. I often wondered what happened to him after pilot training."

The T-28 training was where the students would start their major solo flying, including triangular cross-country flying patterns. Most students soloed after 10 hours of flight time. Brian was the first in his training squadron to do so, followed by the time-honored solo ritual of being thrown into the base swimming pool – flight suit, shoes and all.

A HUMBLING EXPERIENCE

Sometime after he had soloed, Brian became a bit too self-assured and cocky. Late one afternoon before the sun set he got into a T-28, needing to build some acrobatic flight hours to meet solo flying requirements.

"I jumped into the airplane without doing a thorough ground preflight check or visually checking the fuel tanks. I took off and started practicing acrobatic maneuvers. Not too long after becoming airborne, I got a flashing warning light that detected an electrical malfunction. My directional gyro started spinning and soon I realized I was lost. I relied on my training and quickly surveyed the emergency options I could take, asking myself, 'Do you want to press the microphone button and admit to the listening world you are lost? Or, do you jettison the canopy and bail out, saying you had an emergency, hoping everyone would believe you?' "

He had been circling over an Air Force base, but the problem was there were two Air Force bases in close proximity with the other, both very near

Another light-hearted moment in training.
Spence Air Base, Moultrie, GA, 1958.

Moultrie, Ga. One was Moody AFB in Valdosta, an Air Defense Command (ADC) and the other was Turner AFB in Albany, a Tactical Air Command (TAC) base. "I didn't know which was which." The sun was quickly going down and he had not received training for night flying. He remembered the stories of night-flying confusion and disasters. He soon came to the conclusion to hell with his reputation – his life was more important.

"It's OK to admit fault," he confessed. "I'm getting on the radio and have them guide me in." Brian resigned himself to admitting that he was lost and made the call – a tough but honest decision. An instructor and student in the immediate area located him and escorted him back to base. "By the time I landed, my classmates were aware of my embarrassing experience and with unmistakable expressions on their faces were wondering, 'How did you screw up and get lost?' My punishment (so to speak) was to march in all military formations for a week with a fur-lined "piss pot" around my neck, plus standing on a chair in the mess hall flapping my arms with a napkin over my head and reciting the "lost" experience. There was the usual hazing."

"That experience stuck with me and the kind of humbleness you have to accept in life. Eventually, it is going to happen to anyone who flies – military or civilian. I began to view this whole series of events as a test. I knew there were lessons to learn such as: preplan and don't be in a hurry; don't be overly cocky; ask for help when necessary and consider fallback options before making decisions." These lessons from the school of hard knocks became a valuable reminder throughout Brian's life.

Not to brand himself a failure after the fact, he also learned another important lesson. The episode also caused him to rethink simple measures he could have taken, such as setting aside the extra time to preflight the aircraft, to dipstick the fuel tanks and go over critical items instructors had harped on in class about using flight checklists meticulously in all phases of flight.

There would yet be other scary times, such as a near miss while flying solo in a night-time cross-country formation. Cadets were in trail formation at one-mile intervals, following each other. He recalls flying over Dale Mabry Airport in Tallahassee, Fla., and a flight instructor flying overhead asking him if he saw a DC-3 at his two o'clock position. "No," Brian replied. As he was getting ready to bank over the airport, he suddenly saw the aircraft's lights and made a quick turn in order to avert a potential collision. Those two lights from the DC-3 struck the fear of God in his heart, although it was impossible to verify the aircraft separation distance. "I can remember shaking the whole way back to Moultrie. It provided the thought of real danger and having the presence of mind to do what you absolutely need to do. You have to constantly keep your head out of the cockpit during VFR (visual flight rule) flights." There is something about death defying maneuvers that hones a person's ability to make the right decisions.

As these incidents illustrate, there is some element of risk in all situations, whether in a flight training program or life in general. Years later, he would face risks of a different kind, such as leaving a major league airline and going to a small upstart operation housed in three spartanly converted World War II hangars in Memphis.

CONSIDERING A CAREER PATH

Brian was coming to the point in his formal Air Force training where he had to decide whether to fly multi-engine reciprocating aircraft or single-engine jets. For most students, the logical answer was jets because they represented the future of aviation. It was also the tail end of the B-25 as a flight training aircraft. Having finished high enough in the class rankings to be able to choose, he decided on the conservative route and opted for the multi-engine

Brian as an Aviation Cadet, 1958.

route. "I was never overly enamored with single engine fighter (props or jets), but I knew that large aircraft operations might play a part in my aviation future, whether military or commercial." In the late 1950s, jet technology was still being tested and background information on jet aircraft was limited. Multi-engine aircraft were engaged in more applications during this time period – cargo, tanker, bomber, passenger, etc. "In retrospect, my choice of multi-engine over jet fighters was more subconsciously career oriented than the short term thrill of single engine fighters." As it turned out, it was not the most glamorous decision, but was a good choice for his future airline career. It also created an opportunity to learn the operational side of commercial aviation and gain a better perspective into the commercial airline management world.

The environment of a multiple crew cockpit served as an introductory learning experience on how to handle differing personalities in conflict situations. Such lessons became invaluable to Brian, not just in the aviation environment, but later in management roles.

Cargo aircraft were entering a fresh phase of transition. In the early 1960s, the delivery of the first C-135 Stratolifter jet cargo aircraft marked the beginning of modernization of Military Air Transport Service's former all-propeller-driven fleet. The Air Force's newer C-141A Starlifter jet cargo transport flew for the first time at Dobbins AFB, Ga. In the early 1960s, it was capable of crossing any ocean nonstop at more than 500 MPH and could transport 154 troops. It carried a 70,000-pound payload.

THE B-25 BOMBER

Brian's next assignment was for the Basic Flying Training phase in Lubbock in the Texas panhandle. There, he looked out over the tarmac and spotted two training squadrons of B-25 Mitchell bombers, the same types of planes immortalized in the book and movie, *Thirty Seconds Over Tokyo*. That airplane held yet another learning curve for him. For this training he had a military, rather than civilian, flight instructor. There was another six-month period ahead where he was required to pick up 140 hours in B-25 flight time to become proficient in instruments, radio navigation, formation flying and cross country navigation.

B-25 Multiengine Trainer Reese Air Force Base, Lubbock, TX, 1958.

To fly B-25s, Brian knew he had to be in good physical shape. Brute force was required at the flight controls and it was an uncomfortable plane, extra noisy and smelly as well. The rudder and nose wheel steering were not connected. Therefore, if a plane lost an engine on takeoff, the pilot had to immediately stand on the rudder pedal to maintain directional control because the plane would quickly swerve in the direction of the inoperative engines. Flying WWII birds was not then and never has been a fine science. Brian realized, though, that if he could learn to fly such difficult aircraft and pass the appropriate check rides, he would receive the USAF-rated pilots' wings and an officer's commission.

There were a lot of West Point and Annapolis guys among the student pilots in Lubbock in 1958. Brian had tablemates from other nations, including one from Saigon and one from Hanoi. Vietnam was not yet a hot spot and was still known as French Indo-China.

THE IMPORTANCE OF COMMUNICATION

One of the more eventful days for him occurred on another cross country training flight to Harlingen, Texas with a Vietnamese co-pilot. It was a simmering summer day in the dry Texas heat. The B-25 had no air conditioning system, hence, flight suits at lower altitudes created very hot temperatures and the body would sweat profusely. As they gained altitude, however, the temperature in the cockpit would drop and the sweat would turn cold next to the body. This situation could result in perfect conditions to catch a cold, or worse.

B-47 Flight Training Class 59G, Brian Pecon, back row center,
Little Rock Air Force Base, Little Rock, AR, 1959.

The smaller Vietnamese student pilot took the initial leg to their destination. Brian's concern was the co-pilot's ability at 110 pounds to keep the aircraft straight on takeoff if power were lost in an engine. Brian knew intuitively that when advancing full power in a takeoff roll, there is a strong tendency of the B-25 aircraft to swerve to the right until becoming airborne. Correct rudder pressure is necessary to keep the aircraft straight on the runway. The pilot must also back up the throttles to ensure equal thrust on the engines. Fortunately, there was no engine failure, but the takeoff roll was very long and tense. The return training flight to Lubbock was successful, but further reinforced the need for clear inter-cockpit communications – especially with foreign student pilots.

STRATEGIC AIR COMMAND

Prior to obtaining an officer's commission as a USAF second lieutenant, student pilots were given a preference where they wanted to be permanently assigned after graduation. Brian noted that he would prefer to serve in a cargo aircraft in the Southwestern U.S. When the long awaited commission day arrived on Sept. 2, 1958, the coveted Air Force wings were pinned on by his mother and father. "The reward is that you become an officer and a gentleman and get to wear the Second Lieutenant's bars. But more importantly, you receive the coveted USAF pilot wings and become an official Air Force pilot."

The two graduation ceremonies were separate: first, becoming a USAF-commissioned officer, and the second for becoming a rated pilot. "I felt more charged when I received the pilot's wings than I did the Lieutenant's bars."

After graduation, Brian quickly bought a car from a local Lubbock dealer and made the 2,000-mile trip back to Massachusetts. There, he reconnected with Peg and the family and prepared for his permanent duty assignment.

Later in September, he was assigned to the Strategic Air Command. At that time, about 50 to 60 percent of each graduating class went to SAC because it was at the height of the Cold War. Formed in the 1950s, SAC was getting most of the dollars, too. Brian was soon headed for B-47 service at Davis-Monthan AFB in Tucson, Ariz., but only after another eight months of training from October, 1958 until May, 1959.

The B-47 was a plane that required the ultimate of coordination because its three-man crew was not physically located in one single cockpit. Nevertheless, during the early years of its operational career, the B-47 was far ahead of Soviet aircraft and anti-aircraft weaponry. Its certain ability to strike effectively checked the Soviet capabilities and may have prevented a shift in the course of history, according to Jan Tegler, author of *B-47 Stratojet: Boeing's Brilliant Bomber.* The jet ultimately became the forebear of most every plane in the sky, Tegler stated.

In between training and occasional leaves, Brian and Peg somehow made the time to become engaged in December of 1958, a little more than two years after their initial meeting. "The need for a future security blanket was the reason for the excessive delay. We weren't sure what the future would hold during the Cold War period."

BRIAN'S LESSONS LEARNED:

1. Know your strengths and weaknesses and recognize your limitations. Preconceived notions can bias your judgment.

2. Learn the fundamentals first before you tackle the hard stuff.

4

Strategic Air Command Post Korea and Pre Vietnam

(1959–1963)

Brian would now enter a new life, albeit in the same general field. He would ratchet the whole game up quite a bit as he started his duties with the Strategic Air Command and commence a training program that amounted to sheer rigor and precision. The program extended from late 1958 until the middle of 1959.

Strategic Air Command's capabilities were hard won. Gen. Curtis E. LeMay began SAC with World War II era piston-engine airplanes. He and his successors relentlessly drove the men who flew and maintained them, modernizing as they went, to forge the most powerful air force the world had ever seen. This formidable fighting force convinced our enemies and friends alike that we could do everything we said we could do, and nothing could stand in our way. It took time to develop this capability and, once developed, it required the total effort of hundreds of thousands of people to keep it sharp and ready to execute the awesome task placed on SAC – the assured and nearly immediate nuclear destruction of any enemy's capability.

THE COLD WAR FROM A CREW MEMBER'S PERSPECTIVE

"We were constantly training to prepare everyone to be combat crew members in the B-47," Brian said. SAC in 1959 retired its last B-36 Peacemaker aircraft and became an all-jet bomber force. The B-47 had already become a popular and reliable aircraft by this time but the training was grueling. An example of the sobering nature of the B-47 training program was witnessed

Front row (L to R) Capt. Richard Jarvis, Lt. Brian Pecon, Captain Stan Kmiecik, Davis Monthan Air Force Base, Tucson, AZ, 1960.

in a mission over Texas. A 1st Lt. James Obenauf, noticed an unconscious crew member after an in-flight explosion. Instead of ejecting, the lieutenant piloted the B-47 to a safe landing at Dyess Air Force Base, in Abilene, Texas. He received the Distinguished Flying Cross for his heroism. The B-47 also was involved in the first instance of aerial refueling of jet-powered aircraft by another jet-powered aircraft, the Boeing KC-135.

There were four separate training phases involved before a crew member was combat-ready. The first phase was a three-week survival school at Stead Air Base in Reno, Nevada, in the middle of the Sierra Nevada Mountains. Though Brian's arrival to the program was during relative world peace for the U.S., the Cold War was a stark reality with Eastern Europe being overtaken state by state by the Soviets and both sides building up their arsenals and early missile programs. Storm shelters were being built in back yards and the Red Menace was still very real. The Soviet Union had launched Sputnik, the world's first artificial space satellite. It also was a time of the Hungarian uprising that was forcibly put-down by the Soviets. The USAF had just successfully launched the first Titan I ICBM. The two-stage liquid-fueled missile was a formidable weapon. It was to be deployed in underground silos and had a range of 5,500 nautical miles.

SURVIVAL OF THE FITTEST

First, Brian and his fellow crew members had a week of intensive ground school. Then they were prepped for the survival phase, which involved field training in mountainous conditions. Fortunately, for his class the training was staged in the fall and not in the middle of winter. In October, the temperatures were mild during the day but cold at night. Snow had not yet arrived.

"If you had to bail out of an aircraft or were captured by enemy forces, you had to know how to survive." That training equated to a mock imprisoned environment in close quarters. One had to undergo simulated interrogation and suffer varying degrees of mental anguish, though not torture.

"I remember being cooped up in a small black box at one point with the door shut probably for a good two hours with only enough room to squat – not sit. They felt this psychological test would be good preparation in the event of capture. As interrogators hounded us with questions of where we bailed out, they tried to see how much mission-related information you would spill. We only gave our name, rank, serial number and date of birth. Again, I had to look at it as a game as I did the hazing at the beginning of my cadet school underclassman training program. I knew there was an end to it, even though it was really genuine harassment."

An actual survival environment stage was the next sequence after the ground school and imprisonment phases. The teams were given a rabbit, K rations, certain basic survival items and small arms. The group of about seven set out in the woods on their own for six days and went through basic survival techniques staged in "foreign" enemy territory. All the while, they lived off the elements of the land with minimal resources.

Sometime in the late afternoon on the last day, the instructors left them on their own to pursue a nighttime trek to a prescribed location. There were "enemy soldiers" planted along the escape routes, with the objective – not to be discovered or captured during the mock exercise.

"We had to be smart and know, for instance, not to walk along a ridgeline or open clearing where we would be easily seen. If any of us were apprehended, they'd punch your evasion card, resulting in penalty points awarded during the exercise."

Brian and his partner, John Brummit, another second lieutenant, were going from location X to location Y to reach the desired safe destination by midnight or as soon as possible. To the amazement of both, other seasoned and experienced commissioned and non-commissioned officers took more elaborate and indirect routes, but took substantially more time to traverse the course. The two, instead, took a direct route and were the first ones to get to the destination without being apprehended. To celebrate the arrival of all the survivor-trainees, a free steak dinner and $10 in gambling chips were provided by Harold's Club in Reno. Ironically, their stomachs had shrunken so much in seven days, they couldn't finish the feast.

Brian and another second lieutenant, Gary Goff were later given a week hiatus en route to the next ground training phase at McConnell AFB in Wichita, Kan. During the en route trip, they stopped and rented a Piper Cub at Pueblo, Colo. on the premise of keeping their hand in flying. It was a conventional gear aircraft and, unfortunately, they ground-looped the small aircraft because their flight training skills were accustomed to standard tri-cycle-gear aircraft with more sophisticated flight controls. Fortunately, there were no injuries or damage.

B-47 TRAINING

The Wichita ground school involved three months of training with an emphasis on jet engine and airframe systems. The B-47 represented the product of cutting-edge research with an innovative design that incorporated advanced concepts of aerodynamics and propulsion. Its structure encompassed a 35-degree swept wing, six strut-mounted engines, with swept horizontal and vertical stabilizers in a streamlined fuselage. Not only that, its initial climb rate, range, cruise speed and armaments were advanced, as was the cockpit configuration.

Another part of the ground school involved learning the basics of navigation. In a wartime situation, satellites could not be relied upon and no GPS system yet existed. They had to learn to use celestial navigation at night and shoot sun lines during the day for navigation.

Training also involved going through an altitude chamber during ground school where the pilots could actually feel symptoms of hypoxia. Crew members could see their fingernails start to turn blue because of deprivation of oxygen. Obviously, it was considered much better to experience hypoxia on the ground than to miss these potentially fatal effects during actual flight.

For co-pilots only, a one-week gunnery school at Schilling AFB in Salinas, Kansas followed. Two 20-MM guns were mounted on the rear of the aircraft. To operate the guns, the co-pilot's seat had to rotate backwards. The guns had a primitive radar system to scan for enemy aircraft. If the co-pilot saw a radar return on the screen, he could lock on the target aircraft and fire the guns at 1,500 yards, hopefully before enemy aircraft fired first.

Lt. Brian Pecon – Strategic Air Command.

The last phase of training was a fourth and final three-month stint, occurring at Little Rock AFB, where he met his two assigned crew members. The aircraft commander, Capt. Richard Jarvis, had been a co-pilot from Davis-Monthan AFB in Tucson. The navigator/bombardier (Lt. Stan Kimiecsk) was new to SAC and had not been to Tucson.

SAC's policy was to bring all three new crew members together so that the last phase of flight training would be conducted as a crew unit. They spent three months working together – eating, drinking and sharing a dorm as a team. For three months, they flew 100+ hours together with various instructors and learned each other's cockpit and personal habits in the plane. This is where the team members' degree of crew coordination and cooperation became apparent. For Brian, it served as another key primer he would use in various professions in the future regarding close-knit team collaboration on involved projects.

They were well aware of how important crew coordination was because of Lt. Obenauf's episode at Dyess AFB. When an electrical failure occurred in the cockpit and a crew member went unconscious, the canopy was blown, but the co-pilot's ejector seat catapult didn't fire. The co-pilot successfully landed the aircraft and did so without damage or loss of life to any crew member. That was perfect coordination. There were several other challenges with operating the B-47. Crew members had to wear uncomfortable helmets and oxygen masks that were necessary for long-duration flights.

After the B-47 flight training was successfully completed and prior to Memorial Day of 1959, Brian was assigned to Davis-Monthan AFB in Tucson, Az. This seemed like perfect timing for Brian and Peg to complete their wedding plans. Already engaged since December, Brian and Peg decided to marry before he reported to his new duty station. He married his Massachusetts sweetheart, Peg Beattie on May 30, 1959 in Pittsfield, Mass. They had kept up with each other via letters for over two and a half years after their initial meeting at the Labor Day picnic in 1956.

In the intervening years, she and Brian grew in their devotion to each other, mixed in with a hefty dose of patience with military life because of the limited times that he could be on leave from the extensive training pattern. Eventually, Peg grew to enjoy the military life. So much so that when, in later years, Brian was contemplating leaving the Air Force to become a civilian, Peg was very much against the move.

The young couple had a long, 2,700-mile honeymoon from Massachusetts to Arizona. That was an adjustment for Peg who had never ventured far from her New England home and her large Catholic family. In more ways than one, she was going from a New England Spring to a hot Southwestern summer. It was, in effect, a huge transition and the temporary housing only accented the change in environments. Altogether, they made three Tucson moves in the first 18 months of their new life together.

Davis-Monthan AFB was the official graveyard of all military aircraft once their flying lives were over. Brian did flight test duty occasionally for those aircraft (especially WW II types) that were to be sold to foreign governments or other Air Force commands. Ironically, even the B-47 he was then flying would soon be retired (replaced by B-52s and ICBMs). In effect, it was a transitional phase of new equipment production.

Brian & Peg Wedding Photo, May 30, 1959.

This was the nuclear age and each alert bomber had to be loaded with fuel, ammunition, survival equipment and, of course, nuclear weapons – everything necessary to go to war. Alert aircraft had to be capable of take-off within 15 minutes of receiving the launch order. SAC was required to maintain a certain number of crews as always combat-ready 24-7.

World tensions and the improving Soviet capabilities meant that response times had to shorten, and the "powers-to-be" decided to place a large portion of SAC forces on what became known as "Home Station Alert," and to pre-position aircraft at overseas locations on what was called "Reflex Alert," or "Reflex" for short. Reflex duty itself called for flying to foreign locations such as Guam, Alaska, North Africa, Europe and Southeast Asia. This type of duty placed an emphasis on long-haul training and placing aircraft closer to actual enemy targets to be engaged in case of actual warfare.

"There were many heroic sacrifices of flying those distances," Brian recalled. "In mid-December of 1959, our crew had to fly a B-47 nonstop between Tucson and Guam. We had to use No-Doze pills, deal with two refuelings and constantly shoot (celestially) sun lines, not to mention the jet lag. There were no left or right navigation landmarks, just unending ocean." All told, it was a 15-hour and 20 minute flight which never saw darkness.

Alert tour of duty periods were rotated by each aircrew at specific weekly intervals, to take off on a training mission so that both aircraft and crews were always operationally ready – all in accordance with SAC regulations and procedures.

This was also the beginning of the Missile Era, reducing the need for manned aircraft in SAC. SAC actually became the operator/user of these new missiles, but crew members looked at them with disdain. As SAC bomber wings were decommissioned in the 1960s, some crew members were reassigned to missile units, resulting in some unhappy transitions to a non-flying career.

After the successive training was completed, the original crew became combat-ready for Alert and Reflex duties. One more vista for Brian was the possibility of having Select Crew duty in the offing. It was a type of built-in crew incentive system. The original crew of Capt. Richard Jarvis, Lt. Stan Kmiecik and Brian was considered a good crew and they stayed together for two years. However, all SAC crews, (aircraft commander, pilot and navigator) are eventually transferred and reassigned to new crews. Brian remembered,

"It was not unusual for SAC to move crew members around due to sickness, etc., hence, the need for crew standardization. After a while you are mentally ready for a change."

The Select Crew was created by a standardization board that selected the best aircraft commanders, co-pilots and navigators. Brian was assigned to such a crew and went on to work for the 303rd Bomb Wing Standardization Board. This gave him the luxury of not having to pull as much Alert or Reflex duty. His first job there was that of a scheduling officer. Each bomb wing crew member had to get standardization checks (performance evaluations) and Brian's assignment was to do evaluations and administer written and simulator checks, navigational and refueling flight evaluations. Successful evaluations were necessary to maintain combat-ready status.

The day before a flight was scheduled, an entire planning day was required to map out the route, check aircraft weights and balance takeoff performance, and check runway conditions and file flight plans. "I can still recall the length of the runway at Davis-Monthan after all these years. It was 13,645 feet at an elevation of 2,705 feet above sea level. The B-47 required most of the runway on hot daytime flights."

The casual observer and particularly the layman today might wonder why the need for all of the meticulous effort. Well, light years have passed in the world since then. The "Cold War" is officially over, and the United States is the winner; the Soviet Union is no more. However, the threat posed to the United States by the former Soviet Union has been replaced by a myriad of other threats around the world, large and small, but just as dangerous in their own way to our interests.

The United States emerged as the winner of the Cold War primarily due to the capabilities of the Strategic Air Command (SAC). They were so overwhelming that the Soviet Union realized they could not win a direct confrontation. This gave the world the breathing room it needed for the democracies to strengthen and the internal contradictions and inefficiencies of the centralized Soviet planning system to destroy itself from within. Even so, the whole multi-year checkmate standoff was not purchased cheaply. What did the Air Force impart from an individual standpoint? On the positive side, most likely it infused the idea of compliance and working toward goals. There was also the essential teamwork aspect.

ANOTHER TURNING POINT

Brian reached another career dilemma. "Was I going to stay in the military or get out? I was not enthralled with being a crew member of a SAC bomb wing the rest of my life so I set up several criteria. One of these scenarios involved my becoming an aircraft commander, which was not a stretch for me, but I needed to be awarded a regular Air Force commission to ensure regular promotions. At the time, I was a reserve officer. Fortunately, I was offered a regular commission, so two out of three things were in my favor. However, the third criteria did not work out. I wanted a class assignment to the Air Force Institute of Technology (AFIT) in Dayton, Ohio, complete my engineering degree and get on the astronaut track." However, the Air Force had other ideas. They didn't give him a date, but wanted him to go to the University of Omaha for a general education bachelor's degree. That wasn't good enough. After some deliberation he decided to leave the Air Force in September of 1963, despite his promotion to the rank of Captain the same month. "I just came to the conclusion and said - that's it. Within several months of my decision to leave the SAC, I received my discharge date of November 29, 1963."

It was also the fall of 1963 and much had happened in the world since he joined the USAF. The Berlin Wall had gone up. John Glenn made the first full orbit flight around the Earth. That was of major significance at the time since this was a match for the Russian's Yuri Gagarin flight. Gus Grissom's flight was a sub-orbital journey. "To be in the air at the same time as John Glenn's flight was a part of history most aviation types tend to remember," Brian said. "I can't say I recall seeing him fly overhead even at that altitude. It was a day flight. I don't think Glenn was in space more than a few hours, but that was a big deal then."

There also was the Cuban Missile Crisis in 1962 that almost brought the USSR and the U.S. to the brink of a nuclear war. "My squadron, as so many of SAC's other squadrons and bases, went to full-fledged alert status and when practice alert signals occurred, you never knew if it was the real thing until you got the radio message in the cockpit as you started the engines." These planes were fully fueled, loaded with "the bomb," 30 bottles of JATO for a jet assisted takeoff, 20MM rounds of ammunition for enemy aircraft, chaff, and ECM (emergency counter measures) equipment. This was the closest he came to going to war. And it was close.

To offer a major milestone in time context, the assassination of President John Kennedy occurred exactly one week before Brian was to be honorably discharged from the USAF. "There was a major concern that I wouldn't be able to leave Tucson with the family and go back to Massachusetts. Of all things, I was also called up for jury duty in Pima County (Tucson) at the same time. Luckily, the local USAF Judge Advocate was able to have me released from jury duty."

When Brian made the decision in the fall of 1963 to leave the Air Force, the business side of life had more of an appeal than the military. He did not want to fly commercially and his other choices were going back to school or joining his father's business, Boston and Pittsfield (B&P) Transportation Company. The trucking business was based in Lee, Mass., halfway between Pittsfield and Great Barrington, and owned by Brian's father and two other partners. It was the biggest trucking company in Berkshire County at that time. The three partners bought the company around 1950. It had around 50 employees with a fleet of about 35 tractor trailers. They owned the ICC rights throughout New England, New York, New Jersey, and Pennsylvania. This was a very valuable position in the days of heavy regulation (before federal deregulation), and was similar to the airline situation. Brian used to ride with the drivers when he was 16 years old and got to know the operational side of the business pretty well.

Unknown to Brian, his father had no intention of selling his interest in the business to him. Brian recalls with mixed emotions, "I wasn't quite as hostile with my father during this time and he was reaching an age when it was easy to hand over the business. However, when he sold his share of the business, he never discussed selling it with me or for that matter considered me in his decision. He never confided in me about anything." That was quite a blow to Brian and he recalls it with some consternation to this day. However, if he had known his father was selling the trucking business prior to his decision to leave the military, he might have remained in the Air Force until his retirement.

According to Brian, there were two primary reasons why he did not have an opportunity to take the business. First, his father did not want to subject any of his children to the same labor-management dealings he had to endure with the Teamsters Union out of Albany, NY. This, in his father's opinion, was a tough group to deal with. Secondly, Leon could see a potential conflict with his business partners. Even though he served as president and handled most of the sales, all of the partners had equal voices in the business. One partner had all three sons already involved in some facet of the business and the other had one son in the business. Ultimately, the transportation business was sold to a New Bedford, Mass. transportation company, Old Colony Transportation, and Brian moved on to other opportunities.

He applied for a crew member slot with United and American Airlines. Both accepted him and advised him of class assignment dates in a multi-engine jet aircraft. Faced with yet another career decision, he had to consider the options. If he took the airline crew position, he was going to have to be a flight engineer for at least two years, an arduous path that was not appealing. But in the back of his mind, he wanted to be in management, as a result of his brief, but rewarding stint in the USAF. "In retrospect, it might have been worthwhile to take one of those crew member job offers and work my way up the seniority ladder, which would provide a decent living. I also knew mandatory retirement age was 60 and thought when I reached that age and had to leave the cockpit, what would I do? By that time I had made up my mind that I was not going to let a seniority number determine my future career path."

That sent him to the other option – to go back to school. He didn't have many resources so that was a tough decision. He was accepted back to Boston University to pick up his last year and a half of college for a bachelor's degree in aeronautical technology. He knew that as an older student he would have little in common with the other undergraduate students and likely be behind the academic power curve when competing with younger students.

He had made a big decision to pursue the academic rather than the technical, passenger aviation or technical route at this point in his life. It would be only one of many times he would have to reinvent himself during his career.

BRIAN'S LESSONS LEARNED:

1. Decisions must often be made when information is so incomplete that the answer is not obvious or intuitive.

2. Teamwork is the art of joining forces to create success.

5

BACK TO SCHOOL: A DIFFERENT LIFE AND TIME TO REFOCUS

(1964-1967)

Anyone who has any longevity in work experience or in career transition will readily admit that it is not easy starting over a phase in one's life, particularly after years and years of formalized training. But Brian knew that to climb the corporate echelons he had to finish his undergraduate degree. He had been able to rise only so far with the two and a half years of college. Yet somehow he knew he had to overcome this hurdle to have a formal career in management — another new and untried step. Here he was, a married father of two and a captain in the USAF reinventing himself as he decided to accept a new phase of life, schedule and routine. "Returning as an undergraduate at a major public university took a different kind of mindset change," he recalls. "I was enrolled in classes with students ranging from freshmen to seniors. A good bit of it seemed out of place and time. I suddenly had to get used to a new lifestyle and schedule again."

The family was struggling financially, but was able to purchase (with his parents' help) an inexpensive 1,100 square feet house in Brockton, Mass., the home of Rocky Marciano - one-time heavyweight boxing champion.

On a typical school day, Brian would get up, do some class preparation, jump in the car and join the commuting run to Boston. That took 35 minutes to an hour with light traffic back in 1964. He was taking a heavy course load and determined to graduate in August of 1965.

"My goal was then to go onward for the MBA. I had mapped out a version of what I was going to do next." That seemed to be a growing common denominator in his life – reinventing himself and mapping out the next direction without fear of change. He began working on a BS in aeronautical technology at Boston University as he built on the Associate in Science degree he had previously earned.

Brian would go to school through the early afternoon, then run out to Bedford and fly at Hanscom Field. He was involved in the Air Force Reserve and it was a source of additional income. The Reserve world then became a common venue for people finishing military obligations. His unit also was made up of professionals: doctors, lawyers and students. It also kept his hand in the flying game and fulfilled what he saw as his obligation to his country.

At SAC, they practically told the pilots what kind of lead to put in their pencils. Here was a different, more relaxed, unstructured flying world. You could actually kick the tires, climb in the planes, rev the engines and just go.

"I had an experience one day when a young captain friend and I went down low and buzzed my house in Brockton," he says. "It was so low that Peg said that it rattled some windows. In the process, we hit a seagull as we started to pull up. We didn't think about it until we got back on the ground and saw the red gash on the wing tip. The minor aircraft damage was reported to authorities, but no action was taken. There was still an element of bravado in us." That wasn't a typical day, of course, but on the other hand, the Reserve was not a rigid command post situation to which he had been accustomed.

Mix all of this with family life, the exams and papers he had to write, along with physics, chemistry and calculus. It added up to a full slate all around. Amazingly, he kind of enjoyed the frenzied pace. After all, at 27, Brian was still relatively young.

He noticed that classmates in college were not as progressive or proactive, perhaps because he was some seven years older than most of his classmates, and perhaps his military experience allowed him to mature more rapidly. That may be an indicator of his graduating cum laude after a year and a half. Again, not an easy feat for someone who has periodic rumblings in his head that he was taking what appeared to be a career hiatus to continue his journey

Campus Quadrangle – Graduation (L to R) Edwin Cooper, Brian Pecon, and Dale Shumway, University of Rochester, NY, 1967.

forward. What kept him pressing on was the commitment to complete his formal education – a necessary ingredient in the business world. Graduation from BU finally came in August 1965.

NEXT STEP – THE MBA

The next stepping stone came on the campus of the University of Rochester in the fall of 1965, where he began work on his master's degree in business. Brian was fortunate to receive a full scholarship. This school was and is still well-endowed today among business schools, a testimony that it had strong programs then which turned out many successful professionals over time.

Before being admitted, though, he took several graduate school entry exams. His hope would have been to attend local Boston area schools such as MIT or Harvard Business School. He learned that Harvard, for instance, wanted a certain number of people from every state in the country and since he was from Massachusetts, it was saturated with more than its quota of applicants from its home state already. That is when he started examining other schools such as Rensselaer Polytechnic and Rochester, both of which accepted Brian. He knew wherever he attended the MBA would be an important catalyst to his goal of executive management. He eventually opted for Rochester, a two-year program that was extremely intensive and thorough. There, he learned how to research and study; this became the basic bedrock for his future business endeavors.

Brian recalled some difficulty fitting in with folks in academia. The experience was not always positive. "I did not dislike them, but I had to work a little harder than the average bear to get through graduate school." Brian was a C+ or B guy and knew that academics would not be his forte in life. Fortunately, when he was working on his bachelors in aeronautical studies, the "light bulb" came on and he made the Dean's list at Boston University in the College of Engineering for the two years. Advancing to the graduate level, Brian realized he had to work much harder to achieve this goal. According to Brian, "I worked diligently at the University of Rochester to pick up my MBA because suddenly I was surrounded by 'little Ivy League students', primarily feeder school students from Williams College, Brown, Cornell, Colgate, etc. They were all pretty quick." Many of his grad school classmates ultimately went to work for IBM in upstate New York. The professors would often require reading one book a week; however, Brian didn't normally read a book in a week. "I don't remember what my grade point average was," Brian recalled. "It was probably a strong C, but mainly because I did a good job on the production management final term project at the end of the curriculum."

Brian has always had the common sense to approach life's problems from the practical side. This became evident later in life when people began to come to him for advice. They knew he was going to take a pragmatic approach to solving a particular problem. He also had a couple of opportunities to teach, but teaching did not hold any allure for him.

THE CHALLENGE OF SCHOOL AND FAMILY

For extra funds, he worked as a computer lab assistant at the University. This was in the day of punch cards and mainframes that filled large rooms. There, he learned about decision trees and process flow charts. Rochester, too, had well qualified professors in statistics and finance. In the classroom, he learned how to evaluate corporate case studies and how to apply organizational analyses on individual business cases.

Peg also had to go back to work. She took a job with Dynalec Corp., then headed by Tony Schifino in Rochester and worked there for a couple of years to get the family cash flow up to speed. After all, they now had to meet the needs of two small girls who were entering elementary school.

Mrs. Pepper, an older lady, watched the children while Brian and Peg worked during the day. By then, the military experience was fading out of the picture as Brian focused mainly on his demanding classes and chose not to participate in the Niagara Falls Reserve Troop Carrier Squadron which was a sister C-119 Reserve unit to the Hanscom Field Reserve unit. He tried to transfer parts of what he had learned in the military and meld it with what he was learning in the classrooms, hoping it would translate to an actual world business mindset.

As if that were not enough, Brian even worked with Xerox during the summer of 1966 to learn first-hand what it was like to work in the business world. He plied his hand in the program management section of the Information System Division, developing what was called a computer forms duplicator, an early printed version of customized copiers.

"That helped me with a career planning decision and answering the question, 'Do you want to work in a technical environment?' " The love was still there for aviation, and try as he might, Brian couldn't rid himself of that lure. All the while, he expressed some hesitancy of jumping at the first bird in hand as so many graduates do today.

After all, if he had instantly grabbed each bird in the hand, he likely would have stayed in the cockpit. He always had long-term views in mind and how his skills, self-satisfaction and ego might mesh in addition to providing for his family.

Many times, Brian would turn down job opportunities such as Eastman Kodak and Xerox in Rochester. The mentality today of "I'm gonna grab it now!" was not part of his point-of-reference framework. In the 1960s, society was in tune more with a long-term commitment and perseverance. A graduate would join a company for the long haul. Still, that would not describe his nature. Blend in a measure of calculated risk-taking, along with long-term goal setting and one would get a better picture.

By graduation time in June of 1967, it eventually got down to where he was going to work full time. There was no ready-made and obvious place yet for the family to live. There were still basic unanswered questions after all of this.

ANOTHER TURN

Then came a welcome American Airlines connection. Peg's boss, Tony Shifino, was a friend of the American Airlines station manager in Rochester and Brian was able to get an interview for an operations management associate position in either New York City or Tulsa, Oklahoma. An AAL station manager arranged an initial interview with an AAL NY corporate headquarters representative traveling on a spring college recruiting trip to Cornell. He made it through the initial interview and was later invited to go to the Maintenance and Engineering Center, headquartered in Tulsa, which resulted in a job offer. Because of his arduous Boston daily commuting experience, New York City didn't appeal to him at the time, so Tulsa it was.

He weighed working for an operations-related department head in middle management or working with a corporate officer in a staff role, where turnover would be quick and most likely, non-satisfying. Most of all, he did not want to become a staff flunky at headquarters, even for the short haul.

"I wanted a feel of how a business really worked. I always wanted to be directly involved in getting the job done." Airline management was the ticket he was seeking. Thus began another bold march into the semi-unknown. By this time in his life, Brian had established one driving force that he rarely mentioned to anyone, but reflected upon privately. He vowed, "Before I am age 40, I'm going to be a corporate officer someplace."

BRIAN'S LESSONS LEARNED:

1. Learn how to reinvent yourself. Develop a willingness to change and learn to adapt to new environments.

2. Always set high, but achievable goals based on grounded principles.

6

AMERICAN AIRLINES "CAREER DECISIONS"

(1967-1974)

When Brian began work for American Airlines, he did so during a milestone period of American aviation in general. It was the era of the Moon landing achievement (1969) that served as the apex of an ongoing story of imagination, inspired by the science fiction movies and novels of the 1930s. This was the time of America's successive launching of satellites, but also with the ability to develop ones that could observe stars from a position outside the distortions of the earth's atmosphere.

The moon landing rested upon foundations laid by NASA's development of the Project Apollo Lunar Module. Finally, on July 20, 1969 astronaut Neil Armstrong touched his Grumman-built Lunar Module onto the Moon's Sea of Tranquility and announced to the world, "The Eagle has landed." The module made five more roundtrips to the moon and served as the lifeboat that rescued the stranded crew of Apollo 13.

These events served as a larger backdrop to the world of aviation, whether military or commercial, of the 1960s. Brian found himself in the arena of the most preeminent airline in the world. American Airlines at the time was an organization virtually peerless among air fleets and played a major role in the development of the Douglas DC-3, dubbed "Flagship" in the American fleet.

The airline developed from a conglomeration of about 82 small airlines companies through a series of corporate acquisitions and reorganizations. In 1934, American Airways Company - in financial straits - was acquired by E.L. Cord, who renamed the company to its present name. Early in its history, the company was headquartered at Midway Airport in Chicago. Its innovations during this period included the introduction of flight attendants and the "Admirals Club," initially an honorary club for valued passengers that later became the world's first airline lounge at LaGuardia Airport.

The main American Airlines route until the late 1950s was from New York and Chicago to Los Angeles via Dallas. One of the early American Airlines presidents, C.R. (Cyrus Rowlett) Smith, worked closely with Donald Douglas to develop the DC-3, which American Airlines started flying in 1936. After World War II, American launched an international subsidiary, American Overseas Airways (later sold to Pan Am), to serve Europe. It also launched flights to Mexico in the 1940s.

With the introduction of "Astrojet" service in the 1960s, American's focus shifted to nonstop coast-to-coast jet flights, although it maintained feeder connections to other cities along its old route. During the 1970s, American flew to Australia and New Zealand, although it traded these routes to Pan Am in 1975 in exchange for routes to the Caribbean.

Following a financial slump in the 1970s under the leadership of former general counsel George Spater, American promoted Robert Crandall to president, after introducing many marketing innovations including the world's first frequent flyer miles (AAdvantage) and corporate travel card (AAirpass). After discovering several thousand unused CRT terminals in a Tulsa hangar, Crandall ordered them refurbished and given to travel agents, which led to the creation of the first airline-owned agent-accessible computer reservations system.

"For most of the time I was with the company, American was running between the berths of being No. 1 and No. 2 with United Airlines in a very competitive race," Brian said, referring to sales revenue and passenger seat miles. All the rest of the carriers (Eastern, TWA, Braniff, Delta, Northwest, Allegheny, Western, Pan American, PSA, United, Continental, etc.) were far back in the pack. It was also a time when the original senior airline management team was retiring and the next generation of management was stepping in.

Brian's tenure with American also marked the beginning of the wide-body aircraft era in 1970. Not only that, but the airlines encountered the first major airline fuel crisis and the decision of whether to build an American supersonic transport - our equivalent of the Concorde. Congress ultimately killed the supersonic commercial program by refusing to fuel such an expensive venture which had limited transcontinental travel value due to sound barrier speed restrictions over land – much less the significant fuel usage.

THE AMERICAN WAY

Brian hit the ground running in the summer of 1967 absent any formally structured company indoctrination. "I wondered at first – was this normal? I found it was normal for the airline industry." The exigencies of this industry at that moment in time did not allow for such niceties. For instance, there was not even a meeting to deal with company benefit issues. "It was my kick-off to learn what it was like to work in the commercial airline world."

American was constantly locked in the battle for that No. 1 spot as the nation's largest passenger carrier in the regulated airline industry. At the forefront was the desire to remain the industry leader in market innovations and financial performance. There were many operational contingencies from weather to planes breaking down and certainly labor issues galore.

This was a wholly different working environment, competitively, in this time prior to deregulation. Air fares and route approvals took months to approve, a different picture from today's changing commercial airline service world. There was not yet a Southwest Airlines or a discount carrier as we know today. American even had its own in-house pilots union, the Allied Pilots Association, which actually allowed labor issues to be resolved faster than the industry as a whole.

Brian's first assignment: to learn the art and science of daily operational meetings. Everyday was a new world that started with a conference call. "We'd go over how to correct and follow up on yesterday's failures, schedule changes, weather, manpower glitches, material shortages, etc.," he said. "We'd learn of an aircraft that blew an engine in San Francisco, for instance, and how we would round up a spare aircraft or spare engine for the San Francisco to New York flight that day. Another day, there would be blizzards in the Northeast. Yet another day, there would be lack of fuel because a vendor had not serviced the storage tank." It was a world of very quick decision-making and contingency planning – all in an environment kin to a pressure cooker. Communications coordination was crucial. Every decision he made automatically affected many other operations and marketing departments throughout the system. Such pressures in decision-making would serve Brian well as he honed these skills over the years into even more complex corporate and governmental environments.

This became part of his standard operating procedure as he worked as an assistant to the manager of Airframe Overhaul in the Maintenance & Engineering Center in Tulsa. The center moved from LaGuardia only a few years earlier and encompassed some 5,000 employees. "I quickly learned you cannot be in a closet by yourself in making decisions. It was a true tectonic plate shift for me, coming from the military to living in the real world. Nevertheless, that is what I wanted."

In the military world, you are often in the planning and supplementary planning modes. In fact, one might spend a full day planning each military flight. Unless it is wartime, there are fewer surprises on the military side. In the commercial airline business, there is a daily flight schedule to run with passengers, whether there is an urgent and unexpected need for parts or not. It involves a constant daily survival mentality of the corporate kind. "I also realized that yesterday's plan isn't going to hack it today. The majority of what you started yesterday may not apply today." Maybe that is why his MBA figured even more strongly into his hiring than his military background did.

MOVING UP

After his initial 12-month probationary period at American, he was promoted to Manager of Maintenance Planning and Scheduling in June of 1968, and was tasked with coordinating all major maintenance visits, both internally and externally for the airline. Specifically, Brian was also involved in preparing the annual airframe overhaul operating budget, which had to be intricately coordinated with many center operating units, including Engineering, Planning, Purchasing, Administration, Contracts, Finance, Quality Assurance, Line Maintenance, Maintenance Operations Center, and NYC senior staff departments (Marketing/Finance/Scheduling). He dealt with labor issues and the Transportation Workers Union – American Airlines' maintenance collective bargaining unit - not to mention special project assignments.

He had been through military boot camp, but here was corporate boot camp of a another kind and just as intense and certainly more complex. American Airlines' all-jet fleet size varied between 250 and 300 as new aircraft deliveries arrived and older aircraft were phased out. The scope of this work was daunting for a 30-year-old with an MBA thrown into a maintenance operation with five or six airplanes being overhauled simultaneously by various lines of hundreds of workers 24 hours a day.

A typical overhaul would involve an aircraft terminating in Tulsa from a revenue flight on a Friday night. It would be brought over from the terminal that night to a maintenance hangar to be defueled, and to be stripped of all removable components, including the engines, seats and landing gear. Monday morning, about 50-80 mechanics would open all the access panels and inspect everything for airworthiness. All the components were removed per manufacturers' and FAA requirements. This process would take place every four to five years for an aircraft and could normally be done in a week's time, depending on the type of aircraft.

When an aircraft was completed, all systems would be functionally checked, culminating in a flight test. Rarely would it take just one test flight. Typically two or three would be required before being deemed airworthy for scheduled passenger service. Maintenance repairs were very different from manufacturing, because once something is taken apart, other problems often are discovered, hence added costs and elapsed time were difficult to precisely forecast. Quite a task for this budding professional in the airline corporate ranks.

He must have proven himself to the top brass who then put Brian in charge of coordinating all maintenance planning efforts for airframes, engines, and components as Director of Maintenance Plans and Programs. This new responsibility also called for planning preparations for the watershed introduction of 747 passenger service in January 1970 to beat the competition (United Airlines). Pan American Airlines operated the first 747 wide-body a year earlier. It is important to note that American at this time also served as a contract maintenance provider for other airlines, for instance, supporting Braniff's "Big Pumpkin" 747's initial daily service (DFW/HNL/DFW) six days per week. Braniff was not alone in relying on American's maintenance expertise. So did British West Indies Airline (BWIA), Trans Caribbean Airlines (TCA), Middle East Airlines (MEA) and numerous other international carriers. All of the maintenance work American and other airlines performed had to be approved and checked off not only internally, but also by the FAA.

THE NEGATIVE SIDE OF THE INDUSTRY

Also during the 1969 to 1970 time period, American Airlines, as well as the whole industry, had massive financial problems due to fuel costs and load factors being extremely low, something the airlines revisited with accompanying pain some 40 years later. The impact was felt in all divisions and departments of American Airlines, creating very high stress levels during these years.

"This became my first personal encounter with the negative side of the airline industry," he said." I had to terminate over 200 specialist employees (planners, schedulers, inventory control personnel and the like) to reduce our costs and related benefits over a phased one-year period." Initially, the layoffs and terminations were prioritized on a seniority basis, but soon afterward, other criteria were necessary to avoid losing critical skilled employees. The decision to terminate these employees was traumatic for me and was the thing I liked least about my years at American. I was about 33 years old and most of the affected workers were in their forties and fifties and thinking of retirement. It is not something taught in an MBA curriculum. Interestingly, I hired only one person at American in seven years."

Since the space program was whirling at dizzying speeds, American also was involved in planning for the Space Shuttle maintenance/airline support program in conjunction with North American Rockwell. They were teamed together in a NASA design competition with other manufacturing/airline teams for a reusable launch and re-entry vehicle. Those early efforts in the 1970s resulted in today's Space Shuttle vehicles. Brian participated with AAL teams in many of NASA's California and Cape Canaveral field visits before NASA finally selected North American Rockwell as the final shuttle manufacturer – utilizing many of the commercial airline maintainability practices perfected over the years in the airline industry. He was also involved with the conversion of a 747 passenger aircraft to the shuttle ferry aircraft – the one returning the shuttle when it lands at Edwards Air Force Base in Florida. "The performance engineering (weight and balance issues) were challenging because the 747 was never designed to be joined in flight with another aircraft, but it saved many NASA dollars in logistics costs."

BUILDING A TEAM APPROACH

All the while, American's airframe maintenance was engaged in something called the Critical Path Management (CPM) of planning on Boeing 727 airframe overhauls. This effort had as its objective the reduction of time to completely overhaul the industry's first 727s which had been introduced in 1963. The goal was to carry out the work in two weeks or less and reduce the subsequent man-hours and materials costs.

This American Airlines 747-100 would become the shuttle
transporter for the Space Shuttle, Tulsa, OK, 1973.

In concert with this, Brian and his planning teammates were engaged in developing a maintenance control system (MCS) to help organize one of the first totally computer integrated airline overhaul maintenance information systems. This information system applied to airframes, engines, components, labor, materials, subcontract support, and other elements. It took many years of constant meetings with systems analysts and management representatives to agree on a satisfactory approach.

One wondered if all of this couldn't add up to a royal headache or panacea for a company. Folks with so many balls to juggle can get sidetracked if not for mentors helping shine a flashlight along the way. Such was Brian's first boss at American, Garner Miller, who originally came from Memphis. They had a lot in common and hit it off well. Garner ultimately became a senior vice president of Maintenance at Allegheny Airlines (later US Airlines) after working at American. "He delegated a lot to me and we had similar personalities. He was a tough guy to work with, but he trusted me and had confidence in what I was doing."

From time to time, Brian would get to participate in the delicate working relationship between the marketing and maintenance departments. "I knew AAL was very organized, but was able to see in one instance how handling airline passenger marketing was critical. One day, a request came down from corporate headquarters in New York City to put something unique into the rear cabin of the 747 – a piano bar. The marketing dollars were allocated, but Marketing never understood the impact on engineering and fabrication shops to produce the final product. It sounds simple from a user standpoint, but it was a real chore to get those sixteen 747 jumbo jets reconfigured quickly so that passengers would see the piano bar in all aircraft. The traveling public quickly accepted this innovation, which was soon matched by other carriers. The same type of marketing requests would be ordered for never-ending innovations like exterior paint schemes, seat pitch changes and the configuration of seats themselves." In other words, flexibility and responsiveness were always around the corner.

An American Airlines DC-10-10 departing Tulsa, OK, 1973.

ANOTHER TURNING POINT

There was no doubt he felt comfortable being in the "big leagues" with American Airlines. "I didn't have to describe to friends and relatives who I worked for – everyone had heard of AA." At American he had a lot of autonomy, which was a good thing during his early 30s. On the other hand, a challenging aspect of his job was how corporate executive budgeting turned on a dime. "After I thought we had done a superlative planning job on the budget, it all went down the tubes when a 10 percent reduction was needed. It was good preparation for future downsizing events I would soon encounter."

Despite the early excitement and successes in Tulsa, Brian began looking beyond the maintenance and engineering side of the airline world and more toward the operations side. "I actually thought seriously about transferring to Fort Worth where the operations side of American Airlines resided, but again, to move higher I would likely need to be on the pilot seniority list. This would mean another delay, which time-wise, would not be in my best interests."

What would become the next step? Fortunately, his early aviation background, especially in the cockpit, was invaluable experience for operations management. However, management positions in the early 1970s were not as likely to pay as well in the short term as cockpit seniority positions. "I'll never know the financial consequences of those early decisions, but the overall confidence level and significance of my contributions has been well worth the long term decision."

In 1974, after seven years, the obvious career options before me were: to move to American's Flight Department in Fort Worth; to relocate to New York in a senior headquarters staff position; to continue at M & E in Oklahoma; or, to move to greener pastures in the airline world. Was it worth the risk to leave the American Airlines security blanket to follow another unknown path?

BRIAN'S LESSONS LEARNED:

1. Value others' opinions and learn to use them wisely when making decisions.

2. Choose your mentors carefully for they will help shape who you will become.

3. Don't become complacent, even if you are leading the industry.

7

FEDERAL EXPRESS
"THE RISKS
AND THE REWARDS"

(1974-1986)

If we quickly survey the last two decades of
Federal Express among industry giants, it seems
like it was always meant to be the global shipping king. However, if we were to project backward
into time during its early years, we'd readily see
that everything didn't always simply work like the
"Absolutely, Positively" clockwork system that is
now so well established.

Let's take a mental journey back to its nascent beginnings, when this fledg-
ling business formed in 1971 was still in the formative incubator of life. Any
week could spell either a new account with more packages or the precipice of
disaster. We must realize that when Brian went on board with this relatively
unknown enterprise, people across America were still asking the question,
"Federal Who?"

"We have to put ourselves back in that timeframe for a moment, when
the express package industry didn't exist in the early 1970s," Brian said. "The
perceived need for timely, accurate delivery of goods had not manifested itself
yet."

It also was a time when Federal Express, before its name change to FedEx
in 1994, was only open on weekdays with a limited number of U.S. cities
served. Saturday deliveries did not begin until the late 1970s. It also was a period in the company's early history when employees occasionally were asked
to hold their paychecks for a few days. Picture a manual sorting hub before
airline deregulation and a time before the company acquired its fleet of jum-

bo aircraft. Advanced package tracking systems were a figment of the future. Even farther removed from the imagination was an international service or a publicly traded, household name company that would someday employ more than 300,000 people.

Initially, Fred Smith had put up $4 million of his own money and investors eventually kicked in another $80 million. His skeleton staff consisted mostly of former military personnel. This was a stage in the business when station managers and couriers sometimes would use their own cars for deliveries. Employees even were asked to use their personal credit cards for aircraft fuel. Even lesser known is the fact that some of Federal's early business was derived from U.S. Postal Service mail contracts.

A NEW BUT UNIQUE OPPORTUNITY

Brian had worked at American Airlines for seven years when in the fall of 1973 he made another career decision. American at that point was heavily involved in maintenance planning schedules for the newly introduced 747s, but Brian was ready to move on. It was common to get inquiries from other airlines and many of his colleagues at American did move to other passenger carriers as airline growth occurred. "I was the only one who jumped to a cargo carrier, which in itself was unusual as the airline cargo industry was not particularly good."

Having seen an article in Business Week about a cargo operation in Memphis, he recalled, "I wrote a letter to Fred Smith and Art Bass, who was serving as senior vice president of operations." Fred was in his late twenties and had started the business only about a year earlier.

"A month or two later, I got a response back. They were interested in me. I had a personal dare to pursue it and see what would happen." Brian made a visit there in the spring of 1974 and recalls walking away somewhat unimpressed by the operation. There was hardly any comparison to American Airlines. Building No. 2 of three hangars that Federal Express had leased from Memphis International Airport contained Fred's office, and on the surface, it looked like a true startup operation.

After about a month and two visits, Brian got a phone call with a job offer. What they paid was close to what he was making at American, but Fred layered on the "lure" of stock options, bonuses and other company benefits. One had to have faith that those would someday have some real convertible value.

His father replied more soberly to his entreaty: "My father was not very pleased as he could see nothing but a huge company debt, while I was already in a good security blanket situation with American Airlines, " he said. "My dad asked me, 'You want to go where and do what? You have a lot of experience and a respectable position and you want to go do this?' "

Brian's mother had no comment. Peg did not want to move again and sternly warned that she was not planning on working if they moved to Memphis, as she already had a good job in Tulsa and was tired of supporting Brian through the many location changes. This later turned out to be true as she only engaged in charity and church functions once in Memphis, in a professional contribution sense.

After a somewhat awkward discussion with Peg, Brian convinced her that the young company warranted serious consideration. She also agreed ultimately to give it a go, even though it meant moving the family 425 miles from Tulsa to Memphis.

Brian saw opportunities in this new venture, and in spite of the uncertainties, decided to take the risk. He accepted the job in July of 1974 as project manager over the aircraft fleet, which only consisted of 16 Avions Marcel Dassault's Falcon DA-20 jets (halfway through an anticipated delivery cycle of 33). Eight of these were used and 25 new, some of which had remained in the Southwestern desert for two years awaiting a buyer. With modifications, this plane could carry 6,500 pounds over a range of about 1,500 miles. The French parent company was no upstart since it also had made the Mirage series of fighters.

HUMBLE BEGINNINGS

To give an idea of the relative quaintness of the operation and his sea change, three old World War II hangars and the original hub building with one single belt served as the entire company operation. Hangar 6 had been modified and cleaned up for the Maintenance Department, administrative offices, an avionic shop and a Falcon aircraft parts inventory warehouse. There was no budget for office furniture, so most employees brought in personal property. Brian recalled using some of his personal lawn furniture in his office.

"I perceived the differences early on of going from an airline mentality to a non-airline mentality, relatively speaking," he related. "It took a year or two to get used to and it was disconcerting at times. The commercial airline

Early Federal Express Hub, Maintenance Hangars and Ramp, Memphis, TN, 1974.

standard for daily aircraft utilization was eight hours per day or 56 hours per week. Federal Express was using Falcons four hours per day or 20 hours per week – almost a two-thirds difference in utilization." This made him question whether this constituted wise use of a new airline's largest capital investment.

Many other rational people would have walked out the door back then. "You have to remember that I came from a structured company environment at American Airlines with extensive operating plans for equipment and personnel in place."

It took someone like Brian, both structured and creative, to make determinations about what was needed in the system and what could be dispensed with along the way. Innovators not only inject into the picture what is new, but are astute enough to see what is not needed when forging a new model.

"There were no computers," he added. "Everything was manually generated and via telephone. Hangar 7 was terrible and unmodified. Originally, Fred's office was in Hangar 7, where he used an old rug to cover a hole in the floor. Hangar 8 was primarily the engine shop for Falcon teardown and build-

up for engine changes." Later on, the administrative office complex of two floors between Hangars 6 and 7 was completed which included all the senior division management offices and a larger conference room with a reception area on the first floor. The Flight Operations (dispatch, briefing and flight coordination) were added to the ramp side of the first floor.

Little Rock, the actual birthplace and home of Federal Express before it relocated to old National Guard hangars in Memphis in 1973, was still very much part of the organization to the degree that Little Rock Automotive was doing the passenger-to-cargo jet conversions on the small French-made jets. They had been originally designed as corporate executive planes. Brian was quite surprised to discover that there were no uniform tracking methods in place for maintenance schedules. He immediately started to formulate and build the maintenance planning schedules for the new company. A schedule was very much needed because these planes were first used as general aviation jets, but were being plied into service for comparatively more scheduled flight hours per week.

Since the Falcon had limited spare parts to be found on a good day, Federal would rob incoming aircraft for the parts. Paperwork to trace the location of parts was almost nonexistent. An employee whose sole task was to bring replacement parts would make trips from Little Rock almost every day. There also were all kinds of reconfiguration challenges with the cargo conversions. The floors had to be lowered and landing gear emergency systems had to be relocated from the rear to the front of the aircraft. Keep in mind that the Falcon was never designed for cargo use. If there was a glitch in an aircraft's availability on the ramp, it would mess up the hub package sort schedule and that had a rolling effect.

"The Falcon was never built to do what it did for Federal," said Clive Seal, who was a longtime senior pilot at Federal who later became a chief executive of Pinnacle Airlines. "We used it two to three times the number of hours and cycles beyond what it was designed for. As a result, things broke and Brian was involved in changing a lot of the systems on Falcons, making them less susceptible to malfunction, especially with the hydraulics, electrical and fuel systems."

There was, therefore, no way to overstate or underestimate the difficulty of running such a mechanical operation that depended upon inventory control and requisition of parts with all of the extra contingency variables tossed into the mix. The Maintenance Department had to find new solutions weekly. Mesh that type of scenario into a backdrop of also having to orchestrate the scheduling of arrivals and departures of aircraft and staging alterations, and the process could become problematic. But then, Brian liked having a problem he could help solve.

"To utilize a small foreign manufactured corporate airframe modified with American avionics and American engines into a 6,500-pound payload freighter was a risky roll of the dice during a time of surplus corporate aircraft, rising jet fuel prices, an air freight industry going nowhere and overly burdensome, stodgy regulations," he summarized.

Federal Express developed its own flight school in 1972 before Brian arrived and it served a couple of purposes: to prepare pilots to fly the Falcon and to enable pilots to obtain their Air Transport Rating certification for other airline employment. Pilots who flew the Falcon had to pay for their tuition and often used money from the GI Bill to do so. The flight school was one of the only early revenue sources for the company in the earliest time period.

Pilots trained with the Falcon and the FAA remarkably was satisfied with this aircraft that was originally not designed to meet scheduled airline maintenance standards. Additionally, the feds were not sure which way to regulate

Federal Express' operations, classifying it either as a Part 135 general aviation operator or as a Part 121 airline operation.

Nevertheless, the steps were formidable in many senses. "We had to make so many tactical decisions from the get-go, such as orchestrating equipment and sourcing hard-to-find parts for the Falcons."

More than three trips were made to Paris and Bordeaux to purchase critical components for the Falcon jets; these were very expensive in addition to their scant availability. A Falcon tail plane actuator could cost as much as a Cadillac at that time. The corporate aviation world in both Europe and the U.S. used a philosophy of very limited spare components for limited flight usage. "Some corporate aviation manufacturers did not believe in providing airline levels of spare components such as airframe sections, engine parts and instruments, since corporate aviation in general didn't generally anticipate airline flight utilization requirements," Brian explained.

His "reinventing yourself" theme definitely permeated the early stages of this from the ground-up enterprise. It was very different from the well-established standard operating procedures at American Airlines. Brian had to quickly adapt to the nuances of working around a fast-turn service where it was hypercritical to rotate a very small fleet of airplanes five days a week and fulfill delivery promises to trusting shippers.

A CHANGING OF THE GUARD

About that time, the early company experienced a major upheaval in the board room. Executives from General Dynamics (the largest venture capital shareholder), Wells Fargo, CitiBank and others were serving on the board. Gen. Howell Estes, a retired 4-star Air Force general, served as chairman, having come on board in the summer of 1974 with Fred Smith as president. In early 1975, an upheaval was created by business losses of approximately $1 million a month, evoking investors' wrath. As part of the reorganization, the General left and Fred advanced to chairman. Art Bass was made president. Since the General was accustomed to having millions of dollars of military funding to back his decisions, he did not fit the role of an entrepreneur for a private enterprise. A detailed template of procedures suited his senses more.

"The board was very new as well as the operating management, but it was evident that the USAF style - formally structured organization with military policies and regimentation - was not going to function easily in a low-budget package airline that was still in its entrepreneurial start-up phase."

THE LEADERSHIP OF FRED SMITH

"Fred's mind always was out here," Brian said, gesturing with his hands held outstretched beside him. "He was tenacious and thrived on constant change. This enterprise was seen as a fly-by-night outfit initially, but Fred was ready to take on the high-rise, high-reward, new way of doing business. We all worked like crazy in these early days."

"At the same time, Fred was good at selling the service, but we had to have the airplanes make scheduled departures to back the pledges made to customers of a new overnight service," Brian said. The leadership started new game plans that helped the company get onto its feet. Federal started hiring ex-UPS people to accelerate into the courier business.

Fred's go-go maverick management style was something to get used to and his business acumen and quick wisdom most often worked. He just had to get his team on board. Often he might say "Here's what I want to do" as he dove into the middle of a new business plan or pursuit.

For Brian, who came from a more structured mindset, it meant a sea change. Everything he had been involved with professionally had carried a much more controlled environment. Suddenly, there was this unstructured approach. "I wasn't comfortable with a shooting from the hip system and was used to more stable environments. This was like the Wild West. But I adjusted and probably brought in a good measure of discipline to the operation that was needed at the time."

"Fred's mind was always racing four steps ahead. He was incredibly intuitive." Even back then, he was very much People – Service – Profits oriented. That was later formalized into an everlasting credo at the company. "It wasn't just a later tagline," Brian said.

Even amid the upheavals and still precarious early going, the company was able to turn its first monthly profit in May of 1975 ($20,000). Until that point, some monthly losses were $1 million or more. It was a challenge to break even financially because it was difficult to develop the correct features of service and pricing in a package system that was literally changing by each month's flight schedule.

"This key break-even point finally came together with a major reorganization and a settlement of internal battles over pricing and cities to be served, in concert with balancing ground and air schedules with leased aircraft." Indeed, there was no operational manual on the shelf that displayed how to manage a package system in the air and on the ground six days a week, using a 24-hour clock. The one-speed hub belt wasn't reliable, aircraft delays due to weather and parts availability were numerous and courier vans were not holding up to meet pickup and delivery standards. The company looked good out in front, but behind the scenes, it was daily on the verge of "slipping a disc." "The spirit of entrepreneurship was alive and well, but we were too busy to notice," Brian recollected.

"FedEx people have worked tirelessly and dreamed boundlessly to stretch our service capabilities and the scope of our network, stage after stage," said Frederick W. Smith, founder and chairman of FedEx. "FedEx now is a centerpiece of how the global marketplace keeps moving and thriving, but that did not occur by a mere natural progression of an industry. It took a whole lot of sustained efforts by many. All of these efforts led to remarkable results and, if I might say, the challenges involved in moving to the next level during the early liftoff stage of our company promised less certain outcomes. Therefore, any business victory was huge in scale."

"To me, Brian left little in his decision-making to mere happenstance and he planned as much as any good professional or executive who makes a real difference," the FedEx founder added. "It was evident that he had a roadmap for making his career decisions and I believe we can learn much from this type of approach. The tumultuous marketplace in which we now find ourselves almost dictates crafting contingency plans. I am also aware of the vast changes he made in his own career, as well, moving from the military sector to private industry, then into the public governmental sector. He adapted well through the often complex process and taught those who reported to him along the way."

Continuing, Fred Smith said, "His work ethic demonstrated a strong sense of duty, perseverance and accountability that is lacking today. With FedEx in particular, he played a valuable role as we grew the early company, particularly in regard to pilot training and management and in helping us bridge new international agreements. We were able to offer international service connections and product offerings in a timely manner, thanks in large part to the groundwork Brian achieved."

A BETTER SYSTEM OF OPERATIONS

"The need for a control system of operations between the airline, the ground pickup and delivery operations and the hub sorting system was critical and took its toll on employees, management, funding, billing, features of sales and other factors," Brian said. "This took years to perfect, but eventually became the nerve center to reach a system of performance reliability unmatched by competitors." The coordinating methodology also served as a template for formulating contingency plans to assure a 99% system reliability scorecard and in asking customers to ante up on pricing structures.

Who better to work on these systems than Brian and his colleagues. "Brian is a meticulous man," said Clive, who served at Federal Express from 1972 until 2004. "He even seemed to like the detail because he's a numbers person. At the same time, Brian is a big picture thinker."

Clive added that Brian achieves balance by having a good sense of humor. If asked to balance the scales between his being chiefly a people manager or project manager, Clive said Brian's forte would weigh more heavily on the project management side. The year 1975 also brought daily package volumes exceeding 13,000 pieces and revenues reached $60 million. The next year, Federal Express was serving 75 cities. In Brian's early years at Federal, they employed about 1,000 employees. Though shipments would soon top 15,000 pieces a day, full marketing efforts could not be cranked up because of limited aircraft lift capacity on a daily basis. Consider that planes had to stop for fuel en route and there were too many contingencies to do a full-blown nationwide advertising campaign. However, by the late 1970s, Vince Fagan, who served as Senior Vice President of Marketing, used the magic of television to help convince the American public that Federal Express could deliver their packages more quickly and reliably than any other service known. That included UPS, Emery, Airborne, Purolator and others.

"By then, we had the system down to carry a fair number of packages per day, but the pricing was extremely cheap - too cheap. When we raised prices, demand went down and it took a lot of advertising to buoy it up to where it needed to be."

To place the early years of Federal Express into historical perspective, its birth was just a few years before the nation's bicentennial celebrations. 1976 heralded the Bicentennial Year and America made it a year-long celebration. In Philadelphia, a new pavilion had been built to house the Liberty Bell. In New York, the largest collection of tall sailing ships since the invention of the steam engine paraded up the Hudson River with more than 6 million spectators lining the shores. The official basketball of the NBA was now red, white and blue.

At noon on Independence Day, every bell in the country was rung for two minutes. Parades wound through the streets of big cities and small towns. That evening, fireworks lit up the night sky from coast to coast. But these buoyant celebrations on the national level did not induce the kind of vaulting-level booster shot that was needed to propel the still-young company to the next level. That would come in the form of airline cargo deregulation, which Fred Smith and Federal Express supported in a nationwide effort to produce a successful vote. It was not easy by any measure. Keep in mind that until this time, the Civil Aeronautics Board was responsible for the routes and rates or tariffs. Deregulation can never be overemphasized in terms of the radical changes it introduced into the entire industry – the kinds of dramatic changes that Fred Smith knew would be necessary for his full-fledged plans.

THE MOVE TOWARD DEREGULATION

In essence, there was nothing more important than having the flexibility of receiving the routing authority to fly any type of aircraft to any destination without incurring any regulatory delays. That was impossible under the outmoded system of granting route authority for a system initiated in the thirties for both kinds of scheduled air service (passenger and cargo).

The originator of Federal Express started the efforts toward deregulation with a premise of pushing for the deregulation of cargo airlines first, realizing that the passenger segment would be far more difficult. But once passenger airlines, which carried cargo shipments in their bellies, learned of it, they were not too supportive of the efforts. In fact, with their entrenched existing routes and arrangements, they were downright resistant. Not only was the passenger airline industry a formidable opponent on this measure, but the cargo airlines, too. Brian said Emery was decidedly anti-Federal Express, adding that, interestingly, UPS seemed transfixed on its ground equipment without initially taking the approach of building integrated air/truck hubs at the time. (By the 1980s, that UPS picture was resoundingly different as it jumped into that framework in a big way).

"Federal Express single handedly had to become the major lobbying force in Washington that ultimately succeeded in deregulating the air cargo industry," Brian said. "Fred took that responsibility on since we didn't have staffs

Memphis, TN, 1978 – Second 727-100 delivery from UAL –
(L to R) Joe Kuperman, Jack Seubert, UAL rep, Brian Pecon, Ed Karabella.

of people particularly designated to do that. While we were running the system, he was making sure that deregulation occurred. He was an island in the ocean."

"We dramatically changed the way air cargo business would be run in the future," he added. "It was clearly a watershed event. Without deregulation, Federal would not be anywhere close to its present form today and in all likelihood would have suffered immeasurably."

There is definitely an analogy to be drawn between what Fred Smith accomplished during this episode and what Howard Hughes did when he tried to enter the international passenger market with TWA. At that time, the international passenger market was controlled by Pan Am which had the federal regulators and the Congress on its side. Hughes challenged the monopoly "single flag carrier" concept and argued for competition. There were congressional hearings at which Hughes personally insulted members of the committee and eventually stormed out of the hearings, leaving the offended senators, press and onlookers alone in the room.

Fred Smith was just as frustrated, but much more conciliatory, and pressed the case for open competition in the global cargo market. The entrenched carriers who served the market at that time fought hard to keep their shared monopoly, but with the help of three very powerful senators – Howard Cannon, James Pearson and Ted Kennedy – and President Jimmy Carter, the cargo deregulation bill finally passed in November, 1977. More than one senator attending the hearings said that Fred Smith was the best advocate who had ever appeared before the committee. He was passionate, committed, persuasive and knowledgeable throughout this process, according to a counsel to the Senate Subcommittee on Aviation. That committee had the responsibility of drafting the legislation that abolished the Civil Aeronautics Board and opened the door for competition in the air cargo industry.

Less than a year after air cargo deregulation was signed into public law in 1977, it was followed a year later with a similar measure for the passenger airline industry. Federal could then use larger aircraft, schedule them on routes without geographic restrictions and set package rates to match true market demand. Deregulation also lifted the amount of tonnage that Federal's planes could carry and with the help of the initial public offering funds, the fleet immediately began adding the narrow body 727s in January, 1978. "We had to have more capacity, and when deregulation occurred, we immediately took seven Falcons off the West Coast and replaced them with 727s. Plans had been developing over time, awaiting deregulation. It was like getting a key to the Magic Kingdom. Now we could customize our equipment to major cities and also set new rates and service features." One container on a 727 equaled the payload of an entire Falcon.

It is difficult today to discern the marked difference in perspective at that time between "cargo" shipping and "small package shipping" with the latter not even in the business vernacular at that time. Airlines tended to think the big-box cargo shipping and expedited small package systems were the exception and not the rule in the industry. In all of its efforts with government regulators or customers, Federal had to get the newer framework into the public mindset.

PERSONAL PERSPECTIVES

As a lifelong friend and fellow pilot, Phil Irish has a unique perspective on Brian. They shared even more than working together at Federal, where both had joined about the same time. Phil and Brian attended the University of Rochester from 1965 to 1967 (they didn't know each other then) and they went to the same Episcopal Church in Memphis (the setting where they first became acquainted with each other).

"Brian has a sense of adventure and is at the same time very tuned-in to people," Phil said. "He listens to people and is guided by a religious sense of treating everyone well. I would describe Brian as quite a methodical person which might have come from his Air Force background. He has a measure of risk-taking, but isn't a classical risk-taker. He has become more cautious over time and wants to know all the players and facts first before making a decision – all the contingencies and variables. Everyone was impressed by these qualities in him. He exudes a confidence to deal with issues and that served him well at FedEx. In correcting these unstructured environments, he infused structure and knew how to get from here to there."

Indeed, Brian was able to interface with Fred Smith when needed. He was placed in key decision-making roles because he had strong flying and executive experience. This was particularly true when Federal wanted to launch its international business. Brian knew about noise mitigation, night flight operations and related matters, using his negotiating skills with authorities and representatives overseas, Phil said.

An initial public stock offering (IPO) in 1978 started the true marketing onslaught in all U.S. time zones as Federal reached out to more and more cities. $22 million was obtained through one million shares and enabled the company to pursue service expansion to new markets and launch other programs.

It also was at this time that Fred Smith asked if Brian wanted to run Flight Operations. "I had the management background and jumped in. Soon, it was nonstop dealing with pilot-related issues. Our flight hours were increasing and we were changing schedules regularly. We had to map out diversion and contingency plans. We would usually hire new pilots in classes of 10 per month, including minority and female pilots." Moreover, he had to develop a pay structure and a new flight crew handbook to finalize work rules that were similar to major airlines, but without requiring a union contract.

"The task Brian had of managing pilots was somewhat similar to what he had seen at American Airlines," said former FedEx Senior Vice President and Chief Financial Officer John Miller, who would also become involved with Brian in several of his business ventures years later. "At the time, there were some things that Brian developed which had not existed at FedEx. He brought his people skills and project management abilities to Federal and he

Leadership Training Session, (L to R) First row: Don Blasl, Byron Hogue, Mike Pfaff, Brian Pecon, unknown, Andy Merideth, and Gary Bowring. Second row: Frank Maguire, Dick Goldsworthy, John Scruggs, Dave Anderson, Fritz Buechling, Percy Lewis, Bob Gavin, Jim Perkins, and Bob Brown. Heber Springs, AR, 1976.

was able to do it for a company much smaller in scale. That skill is relatively rare," John added. "He was able to deal with change and tough times and handle it well. When you are involved in startups, you are developing new ground and it calls for setting in place new processes. I'd call Brian a versatile manager solving day-to-day management problems. In many instances, he'd solve issues before they escalated into problems."

Pilots were another big employee group mostly recruited from the military. Also, Federal was the first cargo/package airline to recruit and hire female pilots. However, there were very few female candidates that met the qualifications of 1,000 flight hours with multi-engine instrument ratings per FAA requirements. "We had female couriers, mechanics and other skilled employee positions, but few pilots. As we began to hire more female pilots, it changed the complexion of what the airline industry looked like," Brian said. "He and I talked about the need to recruit females and minorities," Clive said. "There were not many out there. We needed to go out there and really look to find

Clive Seal with Brian at Federal Express in 1983.

available and qualified candidates. It was our initiative." Other pilots came from the military reserves, the Tennessee National Guard, Eastern, PanAm, Braniff and the like.

Clive pointed out that Brian was involved in bringing in a new pilot compensation piece, helping make the company a more desirable place for employees to work. Brian became very adept in orchestrating the compensation system and had to be good about budgeting and keeping costs under control.

"Before that time, we pilots felt like stepchildren when around pilots from other companies," Clive added. "We had not been the first choice of most pilots, it is safe to say, and there was a lot of turnover in the early days." Other factors that contributed to the allure of becoming a Federal Express pilot occurred when it leaped the hurdle of deregulation and attained larger aircraft. As the company grew, the pilots became a more cohesive group. It never was just a job before or after, Clive said, it was a mission all along. "We would rally around ourselves."

This time period also marked a juncture in which Federal received the first of its bigger airplanes (compared with the Falcons). "Our operating efficiency and reliability automatically improved and we could still use the smaller planes for newer outlying cities to be added to the system." Still, because Federal Express couldn't get enough properly-sized aircraft, it contracted with independent operators that flew DC-3s (C-47s) and other smaller payload single and twin engine reciprocating aircraft. Using contract aircraft and flight crews from other airlines caused issues with Federal's own flight crews. This issue was never completely settled, but use of supplemental lift allowed the company to expand service in a timely manner, Brian noted.

By the late 1970s, the company had a newly composed board, had gone public and was making an operating profit. The time immediately preceding all of that was daunting and not to be underestimated. "It was a very tough watershed period altogether," Brian recalled. "You had us trying to break even, go public, go international, get deregulation and fight off the competition, all at the same time."

By now, Federal also had developed the spoke and hub system that smoothed out over time. "The hub and spoke concept was new to the industry then, as was our method of package tracking," Clive said. "We also worked to figure out ways to make us impervious to weather situations."

NO LONGER A FLEDGLING COMPANY

With the Boeing 727s came containers which improved dramatically the hub and field station onloading and offloading of packages. Seven containers could fit on a standard cargo 727, more with a stretch version. All of this added up to an operation that had finally achieved the sought-after economy of scale and optimization of flight and ground handling equipment – both for the hub and field operations.

Clive said that specially equipped 18-wheelers that Federal created carried the containers to the aircraft and also doubled as fuel tankers, representing yet another innovation for its time.

In 1981, the industry faced a potential PATCO union air traffic controllers strike. "It was serious for us. All of our flights could stop. The Secretary of Transportation got involved and I participated as the FedEx representative. We had two to three sets of contingency plans of what to do if the air traffic controllers walked." Brian played a critical role by attending the U.S. Department of Transportation meetings in Washington, D.C. alongside the FAA, passenger and cargo airline representatives to determine how the commercial airline system might have to operate with less than a tenth of the control tower and center controllers available. President Ronald Reagan eventually terminated 11,463 controllers and hired or transferred enough replacements to operate half of the normal system coverage. The FedEx contingency plan was used for several weeks.

During his tenure, Brian would see the evolution of the entire flight side, including the transition from corporate to narrow body to wide bodied aircraft, the expansion into new cities and points in Canada and Europe, tremendous changes in technology and the giant shift into a deregulated environment. Not only that, but he witnessed the evolution of package tracking to the extent the industry had heretofore not seen. "We got involved in the monumental idea of tracking every document and package in the system on a real-time basis."

The feeder operation, as mentioned, was not as streamlined as the parent company. This arrangement involved contracts with various companies. Ultimately, Cessna Caravans were purchased and flown by contract crews at outlying locations. It all demanded an open, can-do spirit coordinating both inside and outside crew members. Brian certainly possessed that human relations skill.

Still, the mainline pilots were often not happy flyers. They tired of flying the untypical flight schedules requiring flying at night and sleeping during the day. That would throw their sleep rhythms out of whack and resulted in a high divorce rate among the pilots. It wasn't a very popular job. Brian recalled an early system-wide sales management meeting at the Rivermont Hotel overlooking the Mississippi River when he was introduced as the senior vice president of Flight Operations. The introduction invited a generous measure of good-natured "boos," brought on by the growing challenge of field and flight relations throughout the company. He was learning another lesson in making tough decisions.

GOING INTERNATIONAL

Giant reorganizational steps were taken to focus on three new product lines as major company divisions. As 1980 approached, Federal Express was running Falcons, 727s and 737s. It also started receiving its first DC-10s prior to the Christmas package buildup. (The Falcon would be phased out entirely by 1983 – the same year the company hit $1 billion in revenues). These factors also helped with Federal's first international foray into Canada in 1979. Here was a relatively easy gateway into the international theater since there was not too much to handle in terms of customs or flight operations. After all, it

Senior Executives at Federal Express, (L to R) First row - Jim Reidmeyer, Brian Pecon. Second row -Tom Oliver, Ted Weise, Fred Manske, Dave Anderson. Third row - Mike Basch, Ken Masterson, Jim Barksdale. Fourth row - John Miller, Jim Perkins, Memphis, TN, 1981.

meant extending the flight legs a bit farther northward. "Canada got us going in that arena and it was logical because it was, and still is, our biggest trade partner. We just extended the Falcon flight legs past Buffalo at first. Soon, we connected with seven other Canadian cities. The symbolism it created was significant because we could say, 'Yes, we're international.' "

The Canadian business would grow to the $25 million point in just four years. For a while, Brian was responsible for both International and Flight Operations. When he made the wholesale switch after the Canadian package volume was established, it interestingly represented a shift from something that was then established (Flight Operations) to another start-up environment – the overseas frontier of business.

The foray into international routes meant a complete re-education into pick up and delivery ground systems, including all the connecting and refueling points. The addition of each airport was a process in itself. Initially, Brian helped develop four locations in Europe and three in the Far East. Stanstead Airport in England was the first beachhead in that region back in 1984. FedEx was not the first company to deliver Trans-Atlantic packages in Europe, but it was the first to use its proven hub system there with its own aircraft. Other types of international freight delivery systems that were in use there were very traditional in scope, he said.

At the beginning, Federal would use European licensees for deliveries once packages reached their Euro hub. They became like a franchise with contracts arranged and training for the contractors on how to integrate their own systems with Federal Express. A core group of management was assigned to Europe in the initial stages of the operation.

"Brian showed backbone and could defend his positions," Clive observed in several instances. "It was exciting to be a part of this planning, just as with the early stages of flight operations when we had to make a lot of decisions about procedures and operations," he said.

Freight consolidators were heavily used in overseas freight bookings, particularly on the Pacific side of the equation. At first, Federal acted just as a booking agent aboard commercial airlines. The order of the day involved individual passenger couriers who were paid to book flights and occupy a seat on an airline, checking multiple courier bags they carried as commercial packages.

It was a vastly different picture involved in opening up service between the Asian theater of operations and the European side. The Japanese entrée was arduous and its customs clearance process was notoriously cumbersome. Not only that, but it took a retraining of the mindsets about customer service and priority.

"The old cargo mentality overseas was basically - get it there without the customer hand-holding," Brian said. "I remember going over to talk with our European employees in 1984," Brian said. "There were a few French employees there which required an interpreter. It was awkward, but eventually successful in implementing our People – Service – Profit philosophy. Eventually, we developed unique service by creating an international airbill that improved worldwide customer service standards."

Not only that, but Federal's initiation of the scanning of package manifests not only made this possible, but played into the customer service quotient. Key customers were given their own shipping software so they could track packages, schedule pickups and print shipping labels. To get through U.S. Customs, you had to have this basic package manifest list allowing both domestic and foreign customs inspectors to preview the lists before landing, thus being able to pre-select packages of interest.

It was right in the outset of 1984, in fact, when John Dauernheim not only joined Federal via the purchase of Gelco Express International (where he worked), but also when John was exposed for the first time to Brian's management skills. Corporate types know that the most frayed and warty moments come out of the midst of a merger or acquisition. John said the reverse was the case with Federal acquiring Gelco and that Brian was the chief reason he opted to stay on with the company. And in John's case, he was viewing Brian with scrutiny from the outside, perhaps the hardest lens to view someone.

The Gelco purchase was an important one and one that ushered in the company's European presence in a full-fledged manner. Brian met with the Gelco management group in Minneapolis and with the Legal Department to help finalize the purchase agreement in December 1983. He was well aware of how an on-board courier system could be integrated.

Bud Grossman, the chairman of Gelco, had served on the board with Fred Smith when Federal first expressed an interest in expanding internationally. Gelco had four operations in Europe and three in Asia and operated as a courier company, chiefly for major banks. It had a large express division and agents in place. The packages it tendered all were keyed to weigh less than 50 pounds and they traveled in the bellies of international passenger aircraft with onboard couriers.

Fred talked with his fellow executives about a potential purchase and they agreed it was a way to jump start international. As Federal was doing its due diligence to consummate the purchase, Brian was part of the transition team.

"I remember him asking me after the papers were signed and champagne served, 'John, you're really on our side now; what do you think?' Brian was a true gentleman and put the top management of Gelco at ease," John said. "I could see Brian as a person with warm and open professionalism and to me, he embodied Federal Express so I decided I was in."

After the consummation of the deal, Brian arranged a thorough orientation for the Gelco staff and escorted them to all of the facilities. "It was the most thorough orientation I have ever experienced," John said. "He also gave us an idea of how important Gelco was to the expansion of Federal internationally."

As a whole, Gelco brought to the table international business expertise that Federal initially lacked at the time. John would serve the company until 1993, first as Director of Far East Operations and Sales, then eventually becoming Vice President of Worldwide Operations and Sales.

Of Brian's management style, John described him as being a good leader who was diplomatic and one you could trust. He was a fair in a debate and he would even throw out a challenge or two. He also described him as a bit of a workaholic, going from 8 in the morning to about 6:30 in the evening and taking paperwork home regularly. "Overall, he was instrumental in making Federal a success internationally, with his visions and strategies providing a needed difference. He navigated international laws and labor relationships that were amazing tasks in themselves. He had discipline and integrity and instilled a sense of it there as part of Federal's reliability."

Phil Irish agrees with that assessment and then adds a few notions of his own. "He can see the big picture. Brian is exactly the right person to speak up and say, 'How are we going to get there?' Brian's contribution was that he was versatile, methodical and organized at the same time."

The following year, the company chose Brussels as its European hub (later moved to Paris) and Trans-Atlantic two-day service premiered that summer. But it all wasn't as easy as that. Brian met many times with public ministers and officials in Belgium before the hub was established. He saw that Brussels had an underutilized airport and soon established rapport with Belgian government officials, John recalled. "He convinced them about what this would do for their economy and country, even amid their concerns over potential noise and night operations. Brian convinced Belgium that other companies would come once Federal Express established its European hub there."

"With international, Brian was the man," Phil said. "He was designated by Fred Smith when the international division was created. He took him out of Flight Ops and put him there. Fred grasped the idea that having the right person over there to handle the negotiations was crucial. You need someone with really good business sense, someone who listens and who hears even through translators what seems to be important to those people so you can respond and answer those questions. He also knew what flying airplanes in the middle of the night is all about."

International package volumes stayed low for an extended time, representing just about 3 percent of package volume in the early days, Brian recalled. International would not see its first profitable year until 1993. Even then, load factors on aircraft were lopsided; namely, there was very little inbound volume into the U.S. The early outbound volume to inbound ratio was approximately 9:1. That was because Federal was a household name in the states before it was overseas. Today, that deck is flipsided because the U.S. is buying everything offshore but toothpaste, primarily, from China.

Meanwhile, Federal made the wise move of introducing drop boxes and establishing walk-in Business Service Centers, first in major and then mid-sized cities' business districts.

In 1981, Federal made the critical decision to establish Memphis as a Super Hub with satellite hubs in other parts of the country. The Overnight Letter ramped up that same year and in 1982, Federal Express offered its first 10:30 a.m. next-day business commitments as the order of the day.

THE INTRODUCTION OF ZAPMAIL

In an age when fax machines cost $35,000 apiece, AT&T was the single telecommunications carrier and NEC was the electronics product manufacturer, Federal created the Electronic Systems Division to offer ZapMail, a document facsimile service to replace some of its overnight letter service. Business service centers were opening in urban and high-density office sectors and ZapMail was assured a successful run – at least on drawing boards. Originally the system, which worked through telephone landlines, was cumbersome and slow. In an effort to improve the service, a satellite was launched aboard the Challenger on Jan. 28, 1986. Once placed in orbit, the satellite would receive a signal to send and receive documents from small dishes placed atop customers' roofs. Tragically, the Challenger exploded 73 seconds into its flight, destroying the satellite, but more importantly, ending the lives of seven of our finest astronauts.

Additionally, the timing and influx of cheaper foreign-made fax machines along with the deregulation of the telecom industry eventually sealed its fate later in 1986. ZapMail ended up as a failed endeavor that involved a several

Artist rendering of the first Federal Express flight
simulator training facility, Memphis, TN, 1981.

hundred million-dollar write-off when it was all said and done. This mid-1980s venture was well thought out, but the market timing was unfortunate. ZapMail was introduced as fax machines were becoming less expensive to own and operate and telecommunication regulations were changing.

"There was a large effort by my division to obtain communications regulatory authority in the UK, France, Italy, Spain, Netherlands and Belgium before it became evident that ZapMail was not a go," Brian remarked.

Thankfully, the higher yielding international package service finally took its long-awaited expansion with Western Europe, Canada and the Far East, mainly in densely populated foreign business capitals. Despite the initial customs clearance issues, for the most part, global customers tended to be resilient and patient, eventually receiving quality service through more fine-tuned processes between Federal Express and Customs. That involved many bilateral negotiations, of which Brian was a part. Today, this feature is even more accurate with fast-scanning equipment and tracking of all units at pickup, loading, hub sorting, station arrival and, ultimately, customer arrival points. By 1986, Federal Express was processing a million packages a day.

THE DECISION TO RETIRE

It was in that year that Brian decided it was time for retirement. "It became apparent to me that even though aviation had always been part of my life – the forefront really, apart from the family – that I might have experienced tinges of burnout. Fred asked me if I wanted to help start up another company on the air side. It was an opportunity to stay with the parent company in basically creating a new airlift opportunity for large oversize cargo outside the main regular package system. It was tempting, but too big of a hill to climb from my viewpoint. We would need to start creating something again from the bottom up – different aircraft, maybe a different flight crew seniority system, maintenance support and new airport freight terminal agreements."

There was also a short time from late 1984 until his retirement in early 1986 that International Operations was consolidated under the domestic Ground Operations Division and his title migrated from senior vice president to vice president. There was some disappointment in that, however, that was the period when burn-out was already beginning to sink in and he saw a much larger corporate structure on the horizon and knew leaving Federal was in his best interest.

The most important thing to Brian at this point in time was peace of mind. "I made a conscious choice to leave FedEx," he recalls. "The changing structure of the company during the last couple of years created a lot of stress. I had been through a few wars there. Going from senior vice president of International to vice president had an effect. I also believe my church and faith may have influenced me unconsciously, telling me it was time to leave."

After his departure, another sea change came with the FedEx purchase of the Flying Tigers line in 1989, which instantly brought with it a host of Trans-Pacific landing rights. Meshing the pilot seniority ladders of both airlines, though, was none too easy in the aftermath of that acquisition.

It was all a vast – yet relatively fast-tracked – career journey for Brian himself, going from directing maintenance plans and forecasts to becoming a Senior Vice President over not only flight operations, but also international operations. This provided him with greater authority to help shepherd the company during a critical buildup and development phase of the express package airline. He dealt with the formal structuring and staffing of the flight-related groups to coping with the tremendous expansion in the early cargo deregulation era of the express market – often at the same time.

When he left, he could chalk up a veritable list of accomplishments, including:

- Operationally directed the initial FEC 727-100 flight service in January 1978 in less than 75 days, after congressional deregulation legislative passage
- Planned and developed the initial FEC flight training facility of 60,000 SF with 727 and DC-10 full-scale simulators and visual systems plus associated ground training equipment valued at more than $18 million in 1981
- Hired over 200 pilots in less than two years, increasing the annual operating budget to more than $200 million with over 550 operations personnel
- Acted as primary company representative with the FAA during the PATCO/controller strike in 1981. Assured that company airline operations continued without interruption during the resulting controller layoffs
- Facilitated the acquisition and integration of an international express courier company in 1984 which served as the beachhead of the FEC offshore package network
- Developed and rolled out the initial international express package business in nine countries, increasing sales from $15 million in 1982 to $100 million in three and a half years
- Developed the initial Federal Express customs clearance systems for Memphis, Brussels, London and Tokyo for aircraft and scheduled airlines subcontracted by FedEx

Now, Brian would cast his eyes on more focused enterprises that either were startups or had what he considered a good degree of their potential still ready to be tapped.

BRIAN'S LESSONS LEARNED:

1. Many decisions will not be easy or glamorous. Use sound judgment to make them, rather than basing them on what others think.

2. If financial gain is always the measure of your success in the business world, you may lose what is most valuable to you.

3. In order to survive the greatest challenges, adapt and persevere - even with impossible odds.

8

LEADERSHIP AND CONSULTING FOR MULTIPLE ENTERPRISES

(1986 - 1991)

Brian's planned departure from the executive ranks of FedEx and his consideration of new career options marked a pronounced demarcation of past and future in his career path. It involved delineation much more profound than just starting a new job. Although he did elect to join another relatively new startup operation, it was now in a field outside the orbit of aviation in which he had not only flown, but soared.

SPECIALTY LUBE

At this juncture of his life, Brian was leaving a known for another unknown. To be sure, he was never timid about entering untested ground career-wise, but this next venture represented a whole new wheel to his resume. Therefore, it is not overstating to say that Brian was leaving big business (that he helped grow into the big category) for a much smaller venture. Before he became involved in this still relatively new upstart known as Specialty Lubrication Inc., Brian explored some entrepreneurial options of his own.

"I got very close to buying Olive Branch Airport from Belz Enterprises," he said. Belz is the largest private landowner in the state of Tennessee and had developed Metro Industrial Park some years earlier next to the fixed base operation airport in Olive Branch, Miss. Kemmons Wilson, another real estate magnate from Memphis, had developed the airport as well. Yet another huge Memphis player, Dunavant Enterprises owned acreage on the west side

Brian with Family beside Cessna 310, Spring, 1986.

of the field. Brian was familiar with the turf, having domiciled his twin-engine Cessna 310 that he co-owned with an Arthur Anderson accounting executive and a West Memphis Airport board member. "I am thinking at the time, 'You're retired from FedEx, but a long way from Social Security,'" Brian said. "You need a new business opportunity."

During this period, he was exploring these and other initial options. Fellow former FedEx executive Art Bass helped turn Brian's attention to Specialty Lubrication in 1986, which was preparing to launch a whole franchise network of Duration Lube Centers across the country. Art was a structured, entrepreneurial person and his recommendations carried much weight with Brian. Not only that, but the two had developed a close relationship.

The quick-lube centers were introduced under a three-in-one concept: lube/oil/filter services, Duration product sales and thirdly, the mobile lube service. These franchises initially were to operate primarily in converted service stations, but later, the decision was made to build dedicated quick-lube facilities.

"Art asked if I would be interested in this start-up venture. My initial response was to act as a consultant in the development of a business plan to eventually be the precursor of an initial public offering for a much larger product and service endeavor." He did just that during 1986 and 1987. The experience was initially rewarding and stimulating, as was working within a new industry and a small cadre of management, promoting a product that had several applications. All the while, Brian was able to keep the family in Memphis and use the airplane with his work.

In 1987, Brian accepted a position as executive vice president over Specialty Lubrication's operations. Here would be his first true experience with a start-up venture as an investor, lender and management participant, all rolled into one.

This Memphis-based company placed its first lube center in Memphis on Winchester Road. This was not just any speedy lube mother ship. Specialty

Artist rendering of a typical Duration Lube Center.

Lubrication had behind it a secret formula that permitted its product to bind to internal metal components of industrial and auto engines. This compound eased friction to the point that reciprocating engines could run without seizing hours after the oil had run dry. Additionally, extensive laboratory tests determined that the product, previously known as Slick 50, could operate under higher than normal temperatures and was documented by third-party agencies.

The business (which bought the Duration formula propriety rights in 1986) was founded by a former FedEx pilot and had few competitors compared with the automotive fast lube industry of today. At the time, Jiffy Lube and Valvoline were the only competitors, so it was a relatively freer playing field.

The then-young company enlisted professional race car drivers Mario Andretti and Jeff Andretti (Mario's nephew) to endorse the product. In 1987, Mario Andretti went to the Indy 500 with Specialty Lube's product running through his racecar's engine. It was a watershed moment for the company to capitalize on its publicity machine big time. Unfortunately, one of the fuel computers went out when he reached the 183rd lap and he had to pull out of the race, even though he was in the lead. It was like an early bad break. Jeff

"If Duration could do for me what it does for engines, I'd still be racing when I'm 150."

—Mario Andretti.

I have some good news and some bad news.

The good news is, I've discovered a cure for aging.

The bad news is, it only works on engines and equipment.

It's called Duration Engine Treatment Concentrate. And when you read on, you'll find out (as I did) that it may be the most important thing you can put into an engine since gasoline.

Reduces engine wear in new and used equipment

The reason engines wear down and require costly repairs can be summed up in one word: Friction.

Once an engine's internal surfaces are scored by dirty, gritty oil, your engine loses power, guzzles more gas and can eventually require a major overhaul in order to run at all.

But now, I'm happy to say, a nightmare like this can be avoided with Duration.

Duration fuses a micro-film of protective lubricant within your engine.

And since this layer of protection literally fills and *smoothes* imperfections on an engine's internal surfaces, it reduces damaging friction to incredibly low levels. Even in older equipment.

And, all types of equipment can benefit from Duration— not just vehicles. Backhoes, generators, welders, pumps, lift trucks, etc.

Horsepower at 3,000 RPM

155.6 CBHp *(Before Duration)* — 190.3 CBHp *(After Duration)*

One-time treatment bonds permanently

All you have to do is add Duration with the motor oil on your next oil change.

During normal operation, Duration's formula locks a permanent shield onto your engine's most vulnerable internal parts.

The results can save you hundreds or even thousands of dollars over the long life of your engine.

Prolongs engine life

Considering the fact that the average vehicle sold in the U.S. now costs over $13,000, I believe anything you can do to make it last longer is worth looking into.

That's why I'm telling my friends about Duration.

By reducing friction, heat and wear, Duration can help your engine last up to 50% longer.

Imagine your equipment lasting *years*

longer than someone who bought the identical model, at the same time, but failed to use Duration. That prospect alone sold me on this product.

Incredible protection against mishap or neglect

I drove a Duration-treated car 50 miles *without oil in the engine*. Amazingly, upon examination, it showed no sign of internal damage.

Naturally, Duration doesn't recommend you drain your engine oil and go for a joyride. But it's great to know you have that kind of protection against mishap or neglect. And what I like is that you have that protection for the *life of your equipment*.

More power, Better mileage

Since it reduces friction and heat in your engine, Duration also provides you with more horsepower.

Many people, who have used Duration have reported more than 20% increase in power without any other engine modifications.

And because an engine treated with Duration runs more efficiently, it gets better gas mileage, usually from 2-5 miles per gallon.

This is where I put my math to work. The way I figure it, if you drive 15,000 miles a year and normally get 20 miles to the gallon, and gas is a dollar a gallon, Duration can save you $150 every year in *fuel costs alone.* (I hate to even mention it, but those savings will only go up if gas prices rise again.)

Proven in independent tests

The truth is, I've been around the race track long enough to see a lot of products come and go. So I was naturally very skeptical about a treatment that claims to do all the things that Duration does.

But I've seen the test results from universities and independent research firms around the country. Moreover, I've tested Duration myself.

Time and again it has been proven that Duration works, and works for the life of an engine. And that's why I'm recommending it to you.

In fact, Duration Industrial has a full line of proven products to save you maintenance and replacement costs... not to mention downtime.

Duration has solutions

For problem gear boxes, chain drives, conveyors, air tools, cables, hydraulics, etc.

I just wish I could use some of this stuff on myself, and win Indy in the year 2088.

For more information contact your authorized distributor or call toll-free 1-800-334-7854.

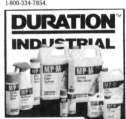

DURATION™
INDUSTRIAL

Mario Andretti Endorsement.

Formula One Racing – Duration Sponsorship for Jeff Andretti, 1986.

Andretti also used Duration in a Formula race in Miami, Florida in November of 1986.

Brian even had his Cessna 310 painted red, white and purple, the Duration Lube Center colors. This could be a true follow-on career for him. The business hoped to do $80 million or more in sales by marketing its consumer products through large merchandise distribution networks such as Wal-Mart's coveted system of stores around the country. There were high aspirations all around.

Not only that, but Specialty Lubrication was on the threshold of going public. It was seen as a marketable commodity. A 50-page business plan that Brian help formulate was part of its testament before the financial world. The company soon grew to 200 or more lube centers by 1987 – on paper – via development agreements. About a dozen lube centers were actually built and functioning.

Yet, for all this buildup, Brian was involved for a crucial, though brief, period in this company's timeline (two years as executive vice president and chief operating officer). In the boardroom, though, he felt pangs of corporate discomfort gnawing in his gut. There were some concerns about the inner financial core of the company, some elements of its prospectus and how it would fare in the coming months. Countless meetings were set among board members and the local law firm of Waring-Cox became involved in the continuous discussions to bring the stock offering to the public market.

Amid the uncertainty, Brian was given the decision at one point to run the company, but after quick deliberation, turned the offer down. "A series of events had killed the IPO deal and its aftermath."

As he recalls today, some part of the decision to not continue Specialty Lubrication was based upon potential legal ramifications and some on his own inner feelings and concerns. These were confirmed in retrospect many years later with a conversation he had with Tony McDuffie, comptroller from 1987 to 1988 at Specialty Lubrication. Many of the investors in the company were monied landowners with connections to the Alaska oil pipeline and market. When the U.S. oil market went bust (including Alaska), it affected the investment dollars flowing to Specialty Lubrication at a time when it was trying to do too much too soon with its retail business, thus squeezing the viability of the venture.

"The gargantuan appetite we had was not likely to become a reality," Brian said. "Not only that, but I might have had to spend too much time in the courtroom in coming years and not be able to manage the crucial startup phase in a manner learned during my FedEx years. A long dormant spiritual aspect of making decisions also entered into the picture as a factor. I leaned toward my inner conscience on this - my heart."

Brian was a seasoned professional. What was this seasoned professional going to do at this juncture, both with Specialty Lube and with his own path? He was not averse to risk, per se, and he continued to try and rework many of the financial problems that were facing the business, but just as the IPO was getting ready to go through, the deal stalled. The IPO materialized legally and it was all set to be committed for final SEC submission where it would go out for underwriter bids. At the last minute, he recalled it was held back from proceeding.

Inaccuracies were found in some of the numbers. Negative vibes pervaded the boardroom. Some board members supported the move to go public at that stage and some did not. At that point the existing private shareholders asked that Brian take the reins and create another parallel company. For Brian to take a major leadership role, he realized he might have to go through a two-year court battle to put the company back on track.

Still, the battle wracked his mind. Here was a man who never turned away from a fight. But tough questions never have easy answers, do they?

The layered perseverance that Brian had built up over half a lifetime was having a battle with the specter of a potential business failure on the horizon. He made the decision to leave Specialty Lubrication in 1988, but stayed on to assist with closing the company in the proper manner. The process involved the difficult task of storing equipment, products, steering a complex legal process and terminating valued employees.

Not long afterward, the publicly facing side of the company closed down. Therefore, the industrial and consumer products marketing effort was terminated. Some of the lube centers continued, however, as did those in Memphis under franchise ownership.

In retrospect, Brian humbly recalled, "I learned from this experience as a whole that not every startup is a FedEx. Art Bass inspired me and we did do a good share of planning the growth foundations for the company; we hired employees and interested some potential shareholder groups. Lube centers were established and we had an excellent consumer and industrial product. In fact, the industrial product had a lot more potential impact in my estimation than the mass consumer or retail market. At the end of the run, this added up to be a new product with bad timing. We tried to grow too fast and didn't have that level of assurance we would need to obtain the capital funding for our expansion plans. We became enamored with recent franchise successes and ran it all up the ladder too fast."

HEAVY MACHINES, INC.

Out of that enterprise, Brian vowed to get back to a more common sense business approach for making decisions. This pragmatic resolution took him to the doors of a man he had also known for a long time, Richard Wilson, Sr., who was running a respectable and rock-solid operation, Heavy Machines, Inc., founded some 20 years earlier. The year was 1988 and Brian was ready for a return to a semblance of business normalcy again.

This transitioning began as a consulting agreement – a common entry denominator in several forays of Brian's. Richard Wilson, Sr., founder of Heavy Machines (HMI) and a friend through Episcopal Church circles, met with him to share some ideas he had about growing his business. They tried to match company needs with Brian's own needs at this stage of his work life (age 53).

This equipment business was engaged in several orbs of industry to develop a well-balanced diversification: inter-modal movement of containers on and off rail tracks, forest product harvesting and mining. At the time, HMI was employing about 220 at multiple service branches across the Southeast and at a rebuild facility in Memphis and was hitting around $45 million in annual sales.

"The business was diversified so that if one industry sector was down, the other sectors could compensate to maintain the needed business levels," Brian explained. "By straddling three distinct major industries, it was possible to balance sales and service between those in the up cycles with those on the downside of the industry growth or those in outright decline."

Service technicians were positioned in the field to maintain the electrical motor equipment and wheel drives. Small branches were set up to support equipment in various southeastern states where client-owned equipment was operated. Communications were difficult, Brian said, and parts support was not always optimal, but the working relationship between HMI and its customers was a key to sustaining successful operations.

HMI had long-term contracts then with Marathon LeTourneau in Texas, almost to the point of being married to them. Over time though, Marathon chose not to change their products and was not being price competitive. For a sales and service organization, which HMI was, it proved to be stultifying for good business flexibility, Brian and the management soon concluded.

"This was a serious issue due to the strong contractual influence on the dealers," said Brian, who worked in the capacity of vice president of contract maintenance services until 1991. "Product pricing and parts support hurt the dealers when negotiating with equipment users."

Wisely, over time HMI brought in other equipment manufacturers which lessened the negative impact of Marathon's decisions. "The other manufacturers' products offered more competitive pricing." Brian learned much from this experience. Despite good leadership qualities and financial foresight in a dealership environment, "Do not leave all your eggs in a single basket and allow terms and conditions of your product and services to be controlled by the manufacturer."

"Good cost controls and field support – even high margins – can be stymied by being contractually tied to one equipment manufacturer," he said. "That also creates a limited market penetration for any of the three major industries."

Even more significantly, though, Brian worked to develop a program called Gameplan. This was a total servicing support program for HMI customers. The support program took a major worry factor from many of their industrial customers who knew that their equipment would be maintained and serviced at scheduled intervals or as needed.

"I took what I had learned in the airline industry and applied it to the maintenance of this large capital equipment and machinery," Brian said. "We established repair maintenance schedules and monitored them so that both our operation and the customers would be the most cost-effective. We accomplished this through long-term service contracts."

This, specifically, was a three-year guaranteed maintenance cost program that used computerized management and teamwork with the customers. At predicted intervals, all major components were overhauled by HMI's Renewed Power Division. A set of daily procedures and checklists for machine operators was established and operating data was reported by the user on a regular basis. It also provided customers with predictable, locked-in operating costs. More than that, performance of components was monitored carefully to anticipate predictable replacement parts. This minimized catastrophic failure and unscheduled downtime.

Brian's Gameplan enjoyed the backing from HMI from the onset and he eventually became vice president of contract maintenance. In the period of the 1990s to 2000, Gameplan represented a large percentage of revenues for the overall company, some 30 percent.

John Miller, who worked with Brian at FedEx, served as executive vice president and chief operating officer at Heavy Machines from 1989 until 1991. At one time, the two even talked about purchasing HMI, but later abandoned that idea due to an excessively high purchase price. Additionally, they saw that it was centrally a family-owned company with successors becoming more involved as time went on. That continuity of family ownership has successfully continued to this day.

"It was a very different operation from FedEx and again, Brian's ability to manage groups of employees became evident, though in a different form," John said. "And in terms of project creation and management, Gameplan was basically Brian's project. He was a kind of growth specialist in taking things to the next level."

John remarked of Brian, "He was a good change manager and had to reinvent himself many times. He was extremely efficient, adaptable and resilient when dealing with day to day problems, as well as looking into the future to avoid problems. He could see the big picture of the company in terms of the role he had. His doggedly persistent nature allowed him to adapt well to a variety of situations. Brian overcame many battles with mature companies as well as startups and used his ability to get involved and manage different groups of people. He also had a knack to take things to the next level. That is a skill many people in business do not have."

Brian learned a great deal about equipment sales, marketing and finance from Richard Wilson, during his experience at Heavy Machines. He also became adept at locating financing opportunities and different markets that led to additional funds," Brian recalls.

His son, Richard Wilson, Jr., who currently runs the business, said the Gameplan program is still in existence and now covers more than the original intermodal/forest product/mining industries. It also covers industries requiring scrap metal recycling, wood and metal grinders, road construction, crushers, pulp and paper machines, mining and tower cranes.

Over time, "Gameplan has made longstanding contributions to Heavy Machines," Richard added. It is still a profit center, a unique feature of the company; the same types of tracking processes that Brian formed are used today. Through such a maintenance program, equipment stays in better and more reliable condition in the end, and it gains greater resale value.

Brian marshaled the needed internal company resources to make Gameplan work, Richard said. He had to cut across the existing organizational structure for individuals to adapt to the new system. When he came into the company carrying an American Airlines, FedEx and military background, it brought management experience, drawing respect and a good measure of credibility.

As the country entered the early 1990s, the nation took a downward trend and HMI embarked on a reduction in their labor force, thereby impacting both management and service employment levels. Brian and John were both affected by HMI's downsizing and began the idea to form a consulting group of their own – M&P Associates, Inc.

1991 was a trying year for Brian due to his business activities and relocating his family to a new home. In addition, his second daughter, Priscilla was getting married in October, and there were ongoing legal discussions with the IRS due to Specialty Lube tax settlement-related issues.

Here's How Gameplan's™ Total Support Program Works:

Gameplan is a three-year guaranteed maintenance cost program that uses computerized maintenance management and teamwork. Teamwork between you and Heavy Machines, Inc., which has sold and serviced heavy equipment for over 30 years. This combination of teamwork and Gameplan's guarantee of excellence offers owners and managers of heavy equipment unparalleled control and significant cost savings.

To realize maximum payoff through Gameplan, key players have assigned roles. Conditioning is also a major factor. Heavy Machines' Service Technicians inspect each machine for configuration and performance standards to match the jobs the machine is required to do.

At predicted intervals, all major components are overhauled by Heavy Machines' Renewed Power Division.

A mutually acceptable set of daily operating procedures and checklists for machine operators is established. Operating data is reported by the user on a regular basis to record machine availability. All aspects of machine operations are covered by Gameplan. A special option even covers engine and tire servicing.

It's a Guaranteed Annual Maintenance Excellence Plan, which gives you a known cost per unit.

Examine Gameplan's features carefully. Then call us to put together your winning team. And let's beat uncontrolled maintenance costs.

Heavy Machines Gameplan Marketing Brochure.

Early in 1991, Brian continued to consult with HMI because of contract agreement changes, so there wasn't an abrupt ceasing of functions. Obviously, it was a good severance, but he needed to look to the future.

RESPONSE COMMUNICATION, INC.

After the Heavy Machines foray, business associate John Miller and Brian were occupied with two ideas during the first six months of 1991. Voicemail communication was becoming more prevalent, as they were told by a mutual friend involved in start-up ventures, and they began reviewing the Telephone Answering Service (TAS) market and industry. "We talked with industry associations and equipment vendors and saw some opportunities in consolidating local small TAS services into larger operations by upgrading new digital equipment coming on the market. Remember, cell phones were not in common use during this time."

Its investment base consisted primarily of physicians and medical agency personnel with pagers. With early stage communication equipment, Response took the customer message information and contacted the doctors by pager. "John said he was led into the idea by a local investment banker whose brother was in the medical field. Shortly afterward, he asked me if I would be interested in the venture."

In August of 1991, Brian and John Miller formed Response Communication Corporation (RCC). It was chartered in Tennessee in December, 1991, consolidating three local TAS units into a new location on South Perkins and Winchester under a facility lease agreement. As venture capital/investor funds became available over the next 15 months, new telephone equipment was purchased, training programs were developed for operator standardization purposes, and personnel from previous companies (HMI and FedEx) were brought in to help with the new systems. Initial employment at RCC was about two dozen.

Most of the customers were medical offices and related agencies that needed 24/7 coverage for medical attention. The highest customer call volume was in early July, 1992. However, RCC's financial performance did not reach anticipated levels, which prompted them to search for more answers. From mid-1992 until the end of the year, unanticipated personnel issues made the operation of the agency awkward. "As a result, John, another telecommunications co-partner and I decided to withdraw our efforts at the end of 1992. RCC lived a couple of months into 1993 and closed shortly thereafter," Brian said.

FOREIGN OPPORTUNITIES TAKE OFF

Another business opportunity was literally simultaneous (time-wise) with RCC, which continued into 1993 and 1994, and which actually paved the way for M&P's Russian ventures yet to come. Not to distance himself too far from the aviation world, Brian and John jointly created a partnership with a commercial aircraft repair operation in late 1992 targeted toward smaller off-shore airlines that needed a large hangar facility operation for airframe-related maintenance. The partnership was in conjunction with a local engineering firm Ellers, Oakley, Chester and Rike (EOCR) during the latter part of 1991. EOCR principal Johnny Chester was soon to be the engineering representative for the yet-to-be promulgated Russian Pskov Cancer Center team project.

M & P's responsibility was not surprisingly on the marketing and planning side of the aircraft maintenance partnership. EOCR already had a contractual relationship with the land developer in Amarillo, Texas. Therefore, it was convenient to help build additional maintenance business under the International Repair & Modification Center of Amarillo (IRMCA), which already had an FAA Repair Station certificate to conduct such aircraft maintenance activity. Brian made a number of trips off-shore, one specifically to the Luxemburg Air Cargo Forum in October, 1992. A newly developed marketing brochure was distributed to many carriers in attendance. This visit served as the basis of meeting other Eastern European and Latvian air carriers as well as Russian aviation representatives who became useful in future Russian endeavors.

In January, 1993, M&P continued with the IRMCA effort and with RCC investor meetings to raise capital, but they no longer participated in the operations. This process continued for the next six months. The following planning efforts absorbed the majority of the time until their first Russian trip in March (15), 1993.

BRIAN'S LESSONS LEARNED:

1. When faced with a setback, learn to be resilient. When you go out on a limb, make sure there is another one to bring you back.

2. Life is full of disappointments; learn to see opportunity at every juncture.

9

THE EASTERN FRONT: TO RUSSIA WITH LOVE

(1992 - 1994)

```
Never deterred by either risk or the unknown,
Brian was about to embark upon one of the most
ambitious turns of his career. Yes, American Air-
lines, FedEx and Specialty Lubrication had their
untried nuances associated with startups, but they
were already at least out of the starting gates.
The next launch pad for Brian and his partners
would take him to the most uncharted waters of
all. The team began work on developing a highly
specialized adult cancer hospital in a foreign
land; one that was only newly opened to the West -
a long-time military adversary - Russia.
```

The re-entry into the international spectrum intrigued Brian, as did the newness of working with the freshly opened Russian frontier. "There was the allure of doing something new in Russia. We wanted to bring help in the form of modern medical technology as well as our share of capitalism in this age of Perestroika. We believed it could be the beginning of something worthwhile."

This foray into the old city of Pskov, USSR (300 kilometers south of St. Petersburg in White Russia), after the dawn of the opening of the age-old Iron Curtain, would occur only in the wake of the confluence of many unusual events. A series of personal introductions paved the way for Brian and John (M&P) to become aware of the tremendous needs and opportunities in Russia. In early 1992, Brian developed a mutual friendship with a Christian Brothers University business professor, Dr. Ben Doddridge. The professor had made numerous trips to Russia creating trade relationships with new entrepreneurial Russian startups, primarily working on a used clothing exchange program in different parts of the new Russia.

It wetted their appetites to consider a similar approach for establishing working relationships in Russia. Dr. Doddridge's presence also gave them access to the university's extensive library system, allowing for research into Russian medical and demographic data. What followed was an intricate series of important introductions that led to the Russian project taking shape.

Brian recalled, "John Miller was contacted by Jane Walters, principal at Craigmont High School in Memphis, through common acquaintances. Subsequently, we met Vladimir Kholunov, a new Pskov student (senior) at the school. Vladimir became involved as one of our translators and his family in Pskov became a vital support element for us on the four trips we later made to Russia."

It was Vladimir who introduced John and Brian to Eduard Solodovnikov, a Pskov business man and ex-KGB officer whose daughter was also attending Craigmont. Eduard was a principal facilitator for meeting government and other business representatives and looked for M&P to establish American business contacts, as much as they looked for him to reciprocate in Russia.

In December of 1992, Brian and John met Ludmilla Pukhlova, a Russian teacher and interpreter who came to Memphis with several Russian high school students as part of a student exchange program. This came shortly after Brian and John Miller, requested Ludmilla to be an interpreter for future group interactions, while she continued to be a teacher and student monitor for the exchange program.

Pskov was selected primarily because Ludmilla and Eduard's family roots were in the Pskov-Oblast region. Pskov covers more than 21,350 square miles with a 1986 Oblast (state) population of about 850,000 and a population of approximately 250,000 in the city proper.

After several conversations with Ludmilla and Craigmont High School principal, Jane Walters, Brian and John became enamored with their story of the aftermath of the Chernobyl disaster among the Baltic States, the Ukraine and Northwestern Russia. In 1986, Chernobyl's deadly winds blew nuclear waste directly in the path of these regions. The livestock, land and inhabitants were largely contaminated with the radiation that poured out of the damaged reactor. Though the Oblast geographic regional of Pskov had less than a million people, there were over 36,000 diagnosed and registered oncology patients there. That was ten-fold the incidence of cancer in the U.S.

Russia was a land with limited domestic competition then and virtually no foreign market penetration. It was in transition from a totalitarian socialist state to a democratic privatized economy. No country of comparable size had ever attempted such revolutionary changes in a peaceful way. The interesting combination created a climate of uncertainty, high risk but also great business opportunities.

Brian was at another crossroads of decision-making. The lure of three factors helped him move forward with the venture. He had extensive experience with international business as Senior Vice President of Flight and International Operations at FedEx, especially within Europe and the Far East. There was a ripeness of the opportunity along with the allure to bring more capitalism into Russia. This, mixed in with the element of humanity in building a cancer treatment center in an area where it would make a marked difference in the population's health, offered a unique chance for M&P Associates. Brian recalled, "John and I were a good team to analyze opportunities because John had a good grasp of relative risk with his financial and administrative background, and I brought my operation, management and marketing abilities. I was cautious too, but perhaps more ready to take on a risk."

THE NEW HOPE EXPERIMENT

By December 1992, enough preliminary data became available to begin the project. New Hope Foundation was born with the assistance of individuals from Washington, D.C., Memphis, the University of Tennessee Medical School and St. Jude Children's Research Hospital. "Our conversations quickly grew into a commitment to put together an evaluation group to explore what it would take to develop an adult cancer center in Pskov. With these ideas blossoming, we developed more individual contacts, local and foreign." These contacts included Dr. Alvin Mauer, chief of hematology and oncology at the University of Tennessee, architect Jim Evans, a partner in the Memphis architectural firm of Nathan, Evans, Pounders and Taylor (NEPT) and engineer Johnny Chester of Ellens, Oakley, Chester & Rike (EOCR). Later on in the venture, international wood tradesman Tom Wilson of International Specialties joined the Russian initiative.

With Ludmilla serving as interpreter, the New Hope group began a series of investigative trips to the Russian city of Pskov, using St. Jude Children's Research Hospital in Memphis as a template. This preliminary working group of Brian, John Miller, Dr. Mauer, Jim Evans and Johnny Chester formed the basis for future trips and development work.

As he was accustomed, Brian worked on the research and the business plan or hospital to be called New Hope Cancer Center. The funding arm was called the New Hope Cancer Foundation. M&P Associates completed 501(c)3 filing for NHCF with the state of Tennessee in early 1993. The group quickly put together an investment package for potential investors that included five Pskov entities: The Cancer Center, the Pskov International Airport, the local timber industry, telecommunications and a major local hotel. The feasibility study was to be an $890,000 effort resulting in a $220 million program (1993 U.S. dollar cost estimates). The initial estimates were based on a 102-bed facility requiring 238,000 square feet at a cost of $69.5 million, including medical equipment. Designers were to be NEPT; engineers were to be EOCR, both of Memphis. The University of Tennessee and St. Jude Children's Research Hospital were to provide health administration and expertise for the venture.

The New Hope team took their first trip to Pskov, Russia on March 15, 1993 accompanied by Jim Evans, Johnny Chester, John Miller and Brian. A few days later, Dr. Mauer joined the group. "During our initial two-week stay, we visited hospitals, two universities and had a continuous dialog with local government and healthcare officials." Another important contact was Jane Myagova who always met the team at the Leningrad Airport in St. Petersburg. She worked for one of Eduard's business concerns, which included furniture and clothing manufacturing companies among other political endeavors. It was Jane who helped set up the Craigmont student exchange program in Russia.

During the trip, the team experienced many travel difficulties due to the country just emerging from 72 years of Communist control. The roads were difficult to navigate, always encountering large numbers of soldiers and state border guards during the journey. In the process, Brian learned a smattering of Russian with some preliminary coaching from a University of Memphis professor. In spite of the difficulties, Brian considered the trip to be successful.

Johnny Chester wrote a daily journal of the trip which he has kept to this day. It paints a picture of an old giant nation struggling to emerge into the new world of commerce by fits and restarts. His observations are poignant, detailed and somewhat humorous. In the journal, he describes a vast dif-

St. Petersburg medical tour – (L to R) Johnny Chester, EOCR; Russian, tour guide; Ludmila Pukhlova, interpreter; Jim Evans, NEPT; Brian Pecon; Dr. Alvin Mauer, Univ of TN Health Science Ctr, 1993.

ference in hotel accommodations compared to the U.S., and reminds us of traditional vodka toasts among newly made acquaintances, cultural nuances and a general eagerness by Russian officials to do business with Westerners. The trip was peppered with numerous unscheduled happenings and requests to make connections with local and regional business and construction interests, courtesy of Ludmilla and Eduard. Part of this was the expected attendance at culturally bonding events, including school dance routines, hot spa/cold spa dips at hunting lodges, a hodgepodge of cuisine that never failed to leave out cucumbers as an ingredient, and quickly arranged meetings with officials and even their extended families. In the spa visit, Brian was the only one in his contingent willing to brave the whole bodily bracing routine of hot spa to cold spa immersions.

Quite remarkably, though not entirely surprising, Brian was so enamored with this round robin greeting mode of making newfound business friends that he was dubbed the honorary grandfather of a new baby girl. This happened after visiting several hours with her family members who also were involved as local business and cultural leaders.

In Johnny's words, the first hotel featured "a lavatory which seemed to almost fall from the wall, shower curtains that were a piece of clear plastic

ПСКОВСКАЯ ОБЛАСТЬ

March 24, 1993

The New Hope Cancer Foundation
P.O. BOX 17066
Memphis, Tennessee 38187-0066

Dear Mr.Pecon

When planning the New Hope Cancer Center we would like yju to take info account sone thoughts we agreed on during our mutual discussions.

1. The Center facility costruction is the responsibility of the Foundation. After the completion of "The New Hope Cancer Center" construction, the Foundation, according to the authrity given to it y the US Government and within the framenork of Russian lans, taking into account the Pskov region administration suggestions^ will transfer the facility to a private non-profit charitable enterprise or a state- operated enterprise.

2. The necessary quantity of land will be furnished to the Foudation at no cost for the purpose of the construction of the Cancer Center. After successful completion of the facility the land will be transferred to a Russian enterprise, chosen according to the coditions in Paragraph 1, for an unliimited period of time.

We hope that the Cancer treatment level of the Center will attract not only Russian citizens from different regions but foreign patients as well Treatment at the Center might be paid for the minimum fees which will ensure self sustaining Center operations.

We believe these recommendations should be a guide for your planning for the Center and be considered in the context of today's changing laws and conditions of the Russian Federation.

Thanks again for your international humanitarian efforts for the Oblast of Pskov.

Respectfully

V. Tumanov
Head of Pskov
Regional Administration

V. Pusakarev
Chairman of Regional
Council of Peoples
Deputies

New Hope Cancer Foundation support letter, 1993.

At Pskov White House, (L to R) V Pushkarev, Pskov Council of People's Deputies; Brian Pecon, M&P; Viktor Chernomyrdin, Russian Deputy President; John Miller, M&P; V Tumanov, Head of Pskov Regional Administration, 1993.

that hung over a cord and a shower head that was a hand-held device." Add to that, some soap previously used by other guests, carpet that dated back to post-World War II, stopovers and exposed piping, and one quickly gets the idea of the amenities. Thankfully, hotel accommodations got better each step of the way. How could they not?

Johnny had favorable comments of several Russian connections. He recalled Ludmilla, who also was a teacher of English in the local Russian school, liked to refer to herself as "Mother Goose" and even cooked the crew a special omelet after they endured an array of meals that raised an eyebrow now and then. Ludmilla, he noted, had gained a bit of notoriety in Pskov and Memphis because of her teaching at Craigmont High School in Memphis. Johnny also characterized Eduard, whose daughter also attended Craigmont, "a very well recognized industrialist" who saw potential in ventures such as his one-time desire to turn a mothballed Soviet factory into a tourist facility.

The New Hope team talked with doctors and local city and Oblast (state) authorities, toured hospitals and quickly reached the conclusion that medical care in the region was not satisfactory to meet the very unusual need. These exploratory missions led to grandiose ideas to provide not only medical care, but forest products and cellular communications industries. It took a great degree of boldness, guts, drive and determination, not to mention that it was very pioneering, risky and exciting.

During 1993, M&P Associates entered the local/national political arena more aggressively. Discussions began with Lucia Gilliland from Governor Ned McWherter's West Tennessee office, Shelby County Mayor Bill Morris, officials from the Trade Development Agency (TDA) and Roy Neal from the U.S. Vice President's office. Another key contact was Doug Buttrey, a knowledgeable Washington, D.C. insider who was helpful in contacting funding institutions and elected officials, especially those from Tennessee. Buttrey later became Chairman of the Surface Transportation Board in the George Bush II years. They also attempted unsuccessfully to see Strobe Talbot, the American Ambassador to Russia.

Constant contact was maintained with Ree Russell for the U.S. Trade Office (Department of Commerce). These introductions soon led to an application for funding from USAID. This assistance would be vital for the survival of the New Hope project. Close ties were also forged in Russia with several prominent private citizens, various government officials and members of the Businessmen's Council in Pskov.

"It became evident to John and me that we would have to become lobbyists in obtaining financing to start such a program and that involved help from the State Department. We met with Tennessee state senators and with Memphis international business consultant Bobby Noles." John Miller and Bobby later became partners in another unrelated business venture. Noles headed a bank for the Saudi government and had business interests in Switzerland with private bankers. The officials they met with included then Senator Jim Sasser (who signed a 1993 letter on their behalf to Pskov) and then Representative Don Sundquist, who later served as Tennessee's governor. Governor Ned McWherter and Shelby County Mayor Bill Morris also were behind the effort on this side of the Atlantic. In Russia, signatories included the Pskov Regional Administration and Peoples Deputies, the Minister of Health of the Russian Federation and the First Deputy Prime Minister of the Russian Federation.

Their second trip to Pskov was in July of 1993. "During this trip, my business attaché case was stolen at the Leningrad Airport. All detailed business transactions, especially the Pskov Airport documents supplied by Aeroflot officials, were lost along with two months of business notes. We learned quickly

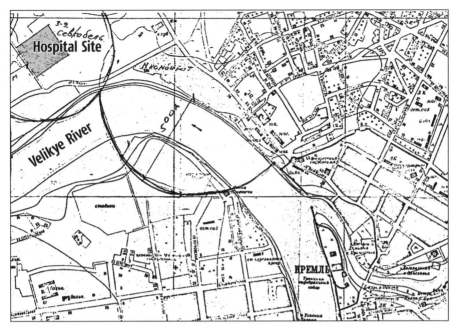

Map of Pskov showing proposed site location of New Hope Cancer Center.

the valuable lesson that Russia was still a very dangerous country despite its newfound political freedom."

Early on, the humanitarian thread was a strong one through the core of the story. On an initial trip there, the team brought a special medication to an ill child in St. Petersburg. A doctor at St. Jude had given Brian the medicine for delivery to a medical partner at a St. Petersburg hospital.

The New Hope team began involving St. Jude along with other local Memphis hospitals (Methodist, St. Joseph, LeBonheur) and out of town organizations such as Sloan-Kettering in New York City and MD Anderson Medical Center in Houston.

In November, Brian and John, along with Tom Wilson and Dick Taft (a Denver, Colo. consultant on airport, marketing and hotel/casino construction projects), took their third trip to Pskov. This included a train trip to Moscow to ensure that Russian airport officials would cooperate with Pskov Airport planning efforts and meet financial institution representatives (American and Russian). "We also visited the Kremlin, Red Square, The Bolshoi Theater and a Russian wood equipment show. In the process, we experienced the scariest taxi ride of our lives."

Brian vividly recalled, "We were running late for an appointment with government officials. Our aggressive Armenian taxi driver took many pinched side streets narrowly missing parked cars, let alone oncoming traffic. The worst part was approaching Red Square, where almost 12 lanes of traffic are used. The driver decided to use the nearest available empty lane (commonly used for oncoming traffic) before the traffic light changed and continued at full speed until the last moment, returning to our proper lane before hitting any oncoming traffic. In the truest game of 'chicken,' he never let up on the gas peddle. It was worse than any airplane ride I could relate to, even as an experienced pilot. No one was killed and there was no vehicle damage, but my heart missed a few beats and my pants barely stayed dry."

Events progressed on fairly optimistic notes with a formal prospectus for investors and even a meeting with Viktor Chernomyrdin, Prime Minister of the Russian Federation. Involved studies were produced which demonstrated that increased numbers of Russians were leaving the nation to receive medical treatment in the West and that basically hospitals were understaffed. Equally important would be the introduction of medical administrative procedures and patient protocols to Russian medical personnel.

The New Hope Cancer Foundation was to serve as the bedrock for the venture. In essence, the Foundation was to contract project management responsibilities with M&P Associates which obtained the Oblast regional authority to proceed with the planning, funding, design and construction of the hospital complex.

After the group drew up a matrix format to study advantages of several sites, categorizing and assigning values in several categories for each, a decision was made. Johnny noted in his journal that a land deed was secured and entrusted to this newly formed non-profit group. (Brian still holds the subject deed approved by the Pskov regional government.) Early in 1994, the planned hospital's 20 hectare site location plans were approved by local government authorities, subject to improving an access road to the site. It was touted to become the first modern cancer hospital in the New Independent States (NIS). Dr. Mauer was very interested in describing it to all as an international facility and not being limited to branding it as a center for that region only. New patients would come first to its diagnostic center for evaluation using diagnostic imaging of various types. Treatment facilities would include a radiation therapy suite and a chemotherapy suite. A completed surgical suite

New Hope Cancer Foundation Agreement signing with Pskov Regional Department representatives and New Hope Cancer Foundation representatives, 1993.

was to be provided as well as inpatient care. A blood bank, pharmacy, food service and medical library were all part of the planned lineup.

Despite the successes and combined efforts of numerous government agencies and influential individuals, clouds began to develop over the project. Cash, credit, and deposit banking operations were very rudimentary in Russia at this time and there was incessant foot dragging by USAID. Funding was sought from USAID which would cover initial construction and equipment needs. Unfortunately, not enough political horsepower and willpower was mustered to sustain the USAID support and this major humanitarian support program was in jeopardy.

In April, 1994, the New Hope team of Brian, John Miller, Tom Wilson and Patrick Greenish (telecommunication specialist and former FedEx specialist) took its fourth and final trip to Russia. Since their first trip to Russia, costs had risen significantly. The exchange rate climbed from $1.00 = 700 rubles to $1.00 = 1,850 rubles in just 14 months. Brian noted, "You can see what was going on with the currency exchange over that short period of time. It was inflation gone wild. This caused us to cut back on basic expenditures such as translators, drivers, cooks and some food and hotel charges. Each person on the team paid their own way including the flight, visa and passport fees. Obviously, our personal pockets weren't that deep. If we hadn't developed the local contacts, the costs would likely have been five to ten times higher depending on whether one stayed in a hotel or an apartment (possibly without hot water)."

Due to the travel costs and minimal Washington support, this was the last trip for the New Hope team, despite the support of many representatives and joint letters of understanding. "We had had good cooperation from the local regional government, but we may have moved too fast and expectations may have been too high," Brian recollected. "If we went over there today, perhaps it wouldn't be much faster, but the legal and banking systems would be improved. The currency would be a little more stable. Obviously, without USAID financial support, the project was finished," he said. "Whether continuous pressure would have changed the landscape, we will never know." Eventually M & P had to back off this Herculean effort and focus on more realistic efforts.

OTHER RUSSIAN VENTURES

Very early in the Russian "experiments," discussions evolved about diversification opportunities beyond the cancer hospital project. "Because of our relationship with Tom Wilson of International Specialties, we began a conversation about establishing a wood products processing company there," Brian said. "We talked with business interests on both sides of the ocean." The idea was to improve their existing system of processing softwood and pulp by providing improved western technology and funding. This was important because the Pskov region produced more than 35 million cubic feet of timber in the 1980s. Softwood statistics also indicated Russia possessed over 57 percent of the world's source of softwood trees. Obviously, this rationale was well grounded and possibly more attainable than the hospital venture, which had become so politically entrenched.

MEMWOOD

"We would supply the technology and the Russians would supply the labor and raw material. We then looked into a joint venture scenario with a major US supplier. They were interested in negotiations and would supply the technical guidance. It was to be done under the business name of Memwood Ventures (a joint venture of International Specialties Inc. in Memphis and

M&P Associates). The objective was to provide dried processed wood products customized to finished U.S. customer specifications.

During this time, more was discovered about duties and tax considerations with a joint venture operation dealing with wood products. They visited many Pskov Oblast rural wood mill production facilities and were featured in an interview by Pskov TV. They also set up business banking credit and shipping arrangements for the Memwood products venture. Trade Development Agency funding for related joint venture manufacturing projects was beginning to look promising.

The potential for the wood products business and also for telecommunications expansion was good. Other business ventures such as selling wood processing equipment (Memphis Machinery) and the joint venture were more than feasible, but required international government support even after joint venture agreements had been signed and approved with board memberships and logistics efforts completed.

"However, when John Miller, Tom Wilson and I analyzed everything, the wood products joint venture didn't seem to be viable all around for us financially. An interesting fact emerged, however, after examining the trees in the Pskov region. They were found to contain too much shrapnel from the bombs of two world wars, which obviously would have ruined saw blades in the cutting process.

Given his Air Force background, Brian could not keep himself from exploring the local airport while visiting Pskov. All Russian airports were part military and part civilian during the Cold War period. The Soviets would often alter the true locations of airfields on regional maps to prevent foes from discovering this valuable information. Another telling sign of Soviet paranoia was seen in the instructions to Brian when he was in the local airport control tower. He was required to only look at the civilian side of the airport and not direct his eyes onto the military side of the Pskov airport complex, which was the home base of The First Red Army Brigade and contained Russian troop carrier aircraft.

There were so many other factors of Russia that also were different to the way of the Western or the free-world enterprise system. For instance, the central planning aspect of Russian living dictated so much, even pricing. There was no concept of real capitalistic marketing practices. The team was dealing with virtually newly created business people who may have had computer, math and physics skills, but who had no idea how to develop pricing for meeting market supply and demand situations. Moreover, inflation of the Russian ruble was changing by the day, although in recent decades, it has been more stable.

RUSSIAN COMMUNICATIONS

The Russian cellular communications industry was in its infancy during this time and overall telephone system infrastructure was lacking as well. If one wanted to make a phone call to the U.S., they had to visit a central communications center in town. Such a privilege was limited to foreign business people with the locals getting the word that it was off limits to them. "You knew you were being monitored, too, and you didn't always get through on these dedicated lines," Brian said. Even fax transmissions were monitored both ways.

Ironically, telecommunications was the third leg of the stool in M&P's Russian venture. Communications of any kind in Russia at that time were very poor if available at all. The international traffic though, as well as the major city switches, were being upgraded by major telecommunications companies in joint ventures with Russia. Brian and John's intention was to install a separate digital switch component for cellular phone service because their information led them to believe there were no digital switches outside of Moscow. This would allow them to generate revenues from data transfer and consumer digital telemarketing services. The local traffic component would replace the existing analog switch, which would double the capacity.

Over time, the M&P team learned that there was no guiding method of getting enterprises ramped up in Russia, especially in its early years as a democratic state. There was too much difficulty, whether legally or otherwise. "You'd almost have to live there a couple of years to get the baseline of work done and I was pragmatic enough to know I was not going to move my family to Russia. I was not daunted much, though, because I had enjoyed success at FedEx and I was ready for another new frontier."

What M&P did have going for it was a cooperative local government that was quite supportive. The local Pskov government felt that M&P was about the right size group for them to deal with and tended to not engage as much with bigger groups who could get outside their grasp of control. The Russians were willing to supply the manpower and raw resources and sought the financial piece and equipment from the initiating enterprise or its backers.

Still, timing became a large factor in the success of these projects. Legal advice was almost nonexistent as Russian lawyers weren't negotiators, but supervisors of legal document preparation. Russian banks were often infiltrated by either ex-KGB officials or the mafia. Labor laws and compensation rates were driven by the black market. Today, the legal and banking systems are more aligned with the western world and vastly improved compared to what M&P confronted in the early 1990s.

There was on the stateside a stymied and often frustrating effort to gain federal approvals through regulatory agencies and international bureaus that purported to help such business causes. "If I had it to do over again, I would have garnered more political and legislative support for these projects in Washington, D.C." Brian said. "We ended up working to fund these ventures out of our own pockets."

Even in today's economy, the improved Russian democratic system of government has not enjoyed the economic growth and success achieved by the Chinese government system over the last two decades. It could be that the Russian business model retains too much of the old Kremlin central planning philosophy and controls.

BRIAN'S LESSONS LEARNED:

1. The logical approach will often be the best course of action, but don't lose your sense of adventure. It's what makes life worth living.

2. Always try to serve others through your work.

10

LIFE IN THE
PUBLIC SECTOR

(1995 - 2005)

With a world of aviation-related work and start-up ventures behind him, Brian embarked on what would become literally a new hemisphere altogether as he entered the public sector. Here is an individual who had helped FedEx rise to its international heights and who had orchestrated the transition between lighter aircraft to wide body jets. A man who had been bold enough to enter the frontiers of nascent Russian capitalism with a humanitarian venture, and one who had also worked on reinvigorating other business enterprises.

It at first seems counter-intuitive that such a veteran of the private sector would go into government work, yet it was precisely that area that he attuned his mind to. It was in the public sector arena that he first became better known to the larger community. Previously, Brian was immersed in the inner workings of American Airlines, FedEx, Heavy Machines, or whatever group he was working with at a given time. At this juncture in his life he wanted to start giving back. He desired to be involved in the governmental side of the development community through the avenue of positional appointment rather than the route of receiving a position through elective office.

Brian first interviewed for the position of Director of the Office of Economic and Resource Development from a field of about 50 candidates also seeking the job. It got down to the last four or five and, eventually, he was selected for the position and approved by the Shelby County Commission and the Memphis City Council.

"Part of what we were looking for when hiring Brian was not to have someone in the role who had been in government all of their lives," said Dexter Muller, (previous Director of the Division of Planning & Development). "We also wanted someone with practical exposure to economic development in actuality. Clearly, there weren't many people that had Brian's background."

Before Brian went on board as Director of Economic and Resource Development, the city's role in economic development was a lesser one than it plays today. Much was left up to the Chamber of Commerce and to the state of Tennessee's Economic and Community Development Department. "The first year with the department, I basically kept my mouth shut and knew I was in a learning mode," Brian said. "With Dexter Muller's help, I was a quick study and we were a good team. He would pick up on something quick and initiate it and I delivered with my sense of follow-through and persistence."

It would involve a mindset change, to be sure. All of a sudden, he was not only accountable to the development community, but to the citizenry of Memphis and Shelby County, Tenn., not to mention several tiers of public sector bosses running the local government. That equals accountability with a capital A. But Brian was as ready for this challenge as he was previous ones. Prior to 1989, there was very little activity in economic development in the city, Dexter noted.

PILOT and MEMPHIS 2005

While working for the Memphis-Shelby County Office of Economic Development for a 10-year period (1995 to 2005), Brian was no administrative caretaker. Rather, he revamped the Payment-in-Lieu-of-Taxes (PILOT) industry incentives program, and effectively convened the One Stop Shop program to successfully court out of town business into Shelby County. He worked centrally with the Memphis 2005 Strategic Economic Development initiative and basically helped grease the wheels of government in order to help make significant business development deals possible. In addition, as an original member of the Emerge Memphis board of directors, an innovative incubator/now accelerator program, Brian helped steer its course, laying the foundation of what Emerge has become today.

Brian served as one of the chairpersons for Memphis 2005, which bears some precursor similarities with the more modern Memphis Fast Forward initiative that was kicked off in 2006. It has performance setting goals reaching out to 2012, is very ambitious and covers realms ranging from economic

"Memphis 2005" Planning Session at Christian Brothers University. (L to R)
First Row: Steve Gilbert (Chamber), Louise Mercuro (OPD), student assistant,
Sherry DuBose (MLG&W), Dexter Muller (OPD). Second Row: Brian Pecon (OED),
Willa Bailey (Chamber), student assistant, Corky Neale (HCD). Third Row:
Lee Warren (CCC), student assistant, Van Oliphant (Univ. Mem), 1996.

development to human capital to almost esoteric areas. It is much more heavily funded by constituent companies and associations than the Memphis 2005
plan, which was public-sector funded with $1.5 million. The county pitched
in most of the funding for the earlier plan. It had no private funding or even
a big push for gaining such support.

"Brian thematically helped Memphis 2005 as it branched out beyond the
city thinking about itself as more than just America's Distribution Center,"
Dexter said. Thus, he helped the committees think through some of the yet
unmined strengths to tap.

"Memphis 2005 was well beyond the classification of a noble effort. It
kicked off a whole new economic model and vision. It was a huge step with
the notion of public-private partnerships. It was a far-reaching plan" Dexter
said.

As co-chairman of Memphis 2005 with Beverly Robertson (now director
of the National Civil Rights Museum), Brian helped steer this program that
resulted in more than $10 billion in investments and some 55,000 net new

jobs. This initiative called for focus group planning sessions involving more than 300 strategic partners and the creation of Jobs Plus, a minority job employment program within the PILOT program. Skill training was a significant factor since job creation was a key element to the heart of that initiative. Its chief goals involved these formalized categories of emphases: Business Development, Job Skills Training, Physical Infrastructure, Minority Business Development, and Amenities & Tourism Growth.

Memphis 2005 planners also were acutely aware and public about the gaps in employment, income, image and investment between Memphis and peer cities. Brian was the man to set up a new, working econometric model for development and incentives. That resulting model gained the confidence of elected officials and private industry.

With the PILOT program, he navigated its needed overhaul as the primary liaison with the Memphis-Shelby County Industrial Development Board. That represented the first major change since Dexter helped initiate the original Memphis PILOT programs in 1988. This revamp involved a full reworking of its policies and procedures and creating the new mechanical processes for its success. The net gain was a responsive industrial community that made decisions based on a strong PILOT program. By 1995 and the following year, this more ambitious PILOT program moved forward. Fortunately, both city and county mayors were supportive.

It could not have come at a more propitious time, because the changes were made among a wave of national economic growth that spawned expansions and relocations of industry from other parts of the country. Companies were making frequent relocation decisions from the Northeast and the West Coast to the Southeast in general. Indeed, 1999 marked the biggest year for the city and county in terms of the amount of available square footage and new projects, Dexter said. "Distribution was hitting a real stride too with upwards of 3 million square feet absorbed in a single year."

Though manufacturing was shifting to Asia, companies still had to bring product through the U.S. aboard trains and interstates and that helped Memphis take off with its confluence of two interstates, six railroads and the Mississippi River.

Frank Ryburn of Millington, who served as chairman of the Industrial Development Board, also provided leadership in regard to economic development during this period, which was significantly augmented with Brian's analytical approach. Together, they proved the long-term value of the PILOT incentive program to government, business and citizens alike, said Sharon Younger, who had been working over time as a consultant with the Chamber of Commerce and with the city to perform cost-benefit analyses for economic development projects and PILOT incentives. These efforts helped to ensure all that the programs were administered fairly and properly.

The very success of the program had curried extra attention, which in turn brought on questions of just how it was handled. That is when Frank and Brian took the time to audit the program and examine every aspect to make sure its components were handled in an optimal fashion, she said. Younger & Associates, her consultancy, was a key ally in combing through data of every PILOT that had been done.

"We were able to show every dollar that had been returned in comparison of what had been provided in incentives," Sharon said. "That helped provide hard data for supporting the program." Brian brought that truly analytic approach in taking the time to examine the program carefully for all to appreciate it, she concludes.

Projects that evolved with Brian at the helm also included the conversion of the 640-acre Defense Depot from the Department of Defense and the twin expansions of FedEx at the global headquarters on Hacks Cross Road and the Information Technology Center in Collierville (together representing about 6,000 jobs). These were joined by other major endeavors such as the Super Terminal Memphis Project for Frank Pidgeon Industrial Park, a five-year expansion program of St. Jude Children's Research Hospital to the tune of some $1 billion and 1,000 added professional medical positions, and others.

"He was front and center with the Super Terminal, CN Railroad and with Birmingham Steel," Dexter confirmed. "His private sector experience shined through, giving him a market-realistic sense of urgency."

In the years that Brian served in this office, more than 150 PILOTs were granted. These included new companies and existing ones that were expanding. Remarkably, most of the PILOT companies have completed their obligations.

"We had an econometric model set up and the company would come in and tell us their wages, capital investment, time to ramp up, etc., and we would plug that into the model so it would tell us one way or another the benefits that would be generated," Dexter explained. Not to be overlooked was the PILOT recipients' requirement to live up to their application require-

Emerge Memphis Facility, Memphis, TN, 2005.

ments on an annualized basis. That accountability, then annual measurements, continues today.

He added, "We also probably kept a number of businesses from leaving Memphis in that decade. This has been verified by the number of companies that have left in the last four years when both legislative bodies initiated PILOT changes. The changes subsequently discouraged growth and resulted in North Mississippi and DeSoto County's industrial growth."

EMERGE MEMPHIS

In 2000 Memphis was one of the only cities in the top 100 populated cities across the country that did not have a business incubator. Memphis Incubator Systems Inc. was formed and later grew into Emerge Memphis. Emerge is worthy of some discussion of its own. The concept was to incubate promising young businesses and urge them out of the nest three years later. Participants would submit their business plans for further workups and their financials. Tenants would cross pollinate effective ideas with fellow tenants. Most were high-tech related startups built on newly emerging technology.

Constantly hungry and persevering for funding, this business incubator has nevertheless succeeded over the years, and Brian was instrumental in helping it secure much of the early Emerge facility public funding that it needed. In the early stages, even when working out of borrowed quarters, Emerge eventually secured some key milestones of success. Long ago it secured its own building near the South Main Historic District under agreement with the Center City Commission through an 11-year buy-back program. Emerge looks for high-growth, focused, early-stage entrepreneurial businesses as tenants. It provides a basic network of support in terms of sales, PR, finance, marketing, and legal input within a like-minded community culture. It also has links to angel investors. Over the past nine years, over 30 companies have "graduated" with over 200 employees and more than $22 million composite revenues. Scant few of its tenants have failed. Currently, Emerge sports two dozen businesses in house with 112 employees; each floor spans 15,000 square feet.

City and County government work at the time was a good experience, Brian said. It also fed into his criteria of giving back to the community. He was able to immerse himself as he was given the responsibility of the aforementioned Memphis 2005 initiative, an ambitious examination of the city's strengths, weaknesses and untapped potential. It was developed as a grassroots effort, though facilitated from the top with the help of Jacksonville, Fla. consultant, Henry Luke. This forward-thinking planning document that resulted from multiple thought-provoking brainstorming sessions represented a full throttled effort that included many people. "It was the most important document since the Jobs Conference of 1979." That earlier conference resulted in the Uniport distribution theme and the "America's Distribution Center" mantle among other accomplishments.

One Stop Shops would muster when an industrial prospect wanted all of the informed representatives of all phases of economic development in one room at one time, ready to answer questions. In a time when companies were more frequently rotating and cities were vying almost weekly for relocation candidates, this proved a leading edge. "We put together what I think was the best decision matrix in the nation," Dexter said.

"We had these meetings almost once a week," Brian said. "The Chamber would bring an interested candidate and we would assemble all the players from MLG&W to the State and Workforce Development. If you were dealing with a company in New England or up north, they'd often say, 'Gee, we've never had this level of cooperation before in one meeting with public agencies.' It would bring everyone together and was widely used."

So many other significant programs transpired during Brian's tenure at the department, including the handover of the Memphis Defense Depot from the Department of Defense to the city and county. The same occurred with the transfer of part of the former Millington Naval Air Station after its transition to the Bureau of Naval Personnel which called for downsizing the former training command property. On a smaller scale, the Shelby County Hospital facility was reorganized by the County for new County offices near the Shelby County Penal Farm property. This says a lot when comparing other cities that have had to mothball government properties that were no longer needed.

FRANK PIDGEON INDUSTRIAL PARK

In the economic development arena, no other industrial tract of land in Memphis and Shelby County held as much untapped potential as Pidgeon Industrial Park, mainly because of its vast size, railroad connections and river port access. Brian became very involved in the Super Terminal Study that looked at ways to optimize a section of the industrial park for a trans-loading railroad facility, an intermodal yard tied in with river barge traffic. This was the vision. Today's presence of Nucor Steel and Canadian National (CN) Railroad would have never occurred if it were not for this focused and wide-ranging study, yet it was a long and unexpected road to land these.

The Memphis and Shelby County Port Commission naturally was centrally involved in the study for the Super Terminal. Rather than a Union Station passenger concept, what was first envisioned was a full-scale yard for all of the railroad lines coming through Memphis - a full-fledged marshaling yard that was owned by the city and county but operated by the railroads. An airline hub mindset was more of the driving model for this railroad application. Brian led the three-year study in the late 1990s to find a way to get all of the railroads into the planned mix.

This concept didn't ultimately get traction, through no fault of the master planners. Burlington Northern-Santa Fe, which had a giant intermodal yard already in southeast Memphis, decided to expand its existing site to accommodate 1 million lifts per year. Union Pacific, the other primary east-west railroad, elected to build a new intermodal terminal in Marion, Ark. due to immediate growing traffic demands. And other railroads didn't jump at the idea of getting together on a multi-enterprise basis with fellow railroads. This also was a time of national consolidations and flux across the board with railroad systems.

As it turned out, despite valiant efforts, it was extremely difficult to get anything going for a multi-enterprise railroad system here, agreed Don McCrory and Randy Richardson, who together lead the Memphis-Shelby County Port Commission. That airline hub mindset evidently didn't drive decisions for different railroads. In the end, Canadian National, which owned the FPIP trackage rights, moved a major rail yard to the industrial park.

This dovetailed into the decision of Birmingham Steel to respond to a PILOT, while also being attracted

Office of Economic Development, Brian Pecon with Shelby County, TN map, 2004.

by the river harbor and utility connections. All of the above resulted in Birmingham Steel making the relocation decision to Pidgeon Industrial Park. The harbor was dredged out already and as a steel mill, it needed water access for shipping. MLGW and TVA stepped forward with an electrical power station and Birmingham Steel made a $200 million investment in 1996 to construct a steel mill at the industrial park.

Over a relatively short time, however, Birmingham Steel ran into trouble during the steel industry downturn. It was an ironic turn of events because everything from the PILOT to the One Stop Shop had worked. Technical labor was coming and workforce development efforts were brought together to make everything happen at the state and local level. The rail extension was attained and MLGW made the promised improvements. State funds were also put in place for training programs. "Birmingham ran out of funding and tried to get into too many things too quickly and were not able to sustain themselves," Brian said.

All would not be for naught, however, through an unexpected chain of events. Nucor, which organizationally took over Birmingham Steel, would nest in the very facility that had closed down. Not only that, Nucor significantly enlarged the footprint of the steel mill, creating in essence an entirely new facility of its own.

Don McCrory and Randy Richardson were able to dissect much of the Birmingham Steel scenario from their office's perspective. The PILOT application was underway by 1997. The industrial park was in the second phase of the Memphis Harbor Project that really stemmed back to the 1940s. Levees were completed by the mid 1960s, creating a whole flood protected industrial area over time, Don explained. Presidents Island had constituted the first phase of that Harbor Project and was built on time and on budget.

Frank Pigeon Industrial Park was originally intended as backup land when Presidents Island reached capacity. "The land was inventory. We viewed it as an area that could accommodate very large industries. It was protected for that reason too," Don said.

By 1982, Memphis found itself in the slow period the country was experiencing as a whole. That turned around in the late 1980s and by the early 1990s, Presidents Island began to fill up. That turned the focus more upon Pigeon Industrial Park, especially when big industrial projects were being courted.

"Frequently, we would get people coming in to look at large sites," Don said. The first choice would be to have a tenant lease the land; if it didn't want that option, the land could be sold. Until Birmingham Steel came along, there was no good access into the interior property of Pigeon Industrial. It received the one-stop-shop treatment and received a 15-year Industrial Development Board-approved PILOT, which was the maximum PILOT term. When the plan was built on a "Greenfield" site, it covered 500 acres. Birmingham Steel purchased the property and placed an option on another tract just as large. The location next to the river with the rail connection was just what it sought to ship both inbound and outbound materials.

"We built out the harbor and the State of Tennessee built the highway, with MLGW meeting the electrical upgrade requirement for the mill's new electrical arc furnaces," Don said. "The rail yard went in and we built a dock." Birmingham Steel operated out of its $200 million facility with some 250 employees for about three years. It ultimately reached about half its capacity.

Everything worked very aggressively and perhaps the plant tried to do too much too fast. The demand was there for its steel billets, made to bar quality and used in the automotive industry for drive shafts and cam shafts.

The dramatic changes in the steel industry with the embargo caused hundreds of steel mills to go bankrupt. Nucor bought Birmingham Steel not long afterward and they didn't realize initially what they really had in Memphis, Don commented. "They later told us, 'We love this location and should have even built our South Carolina facility here.' "

It was three years after acquiring Birmingham Steel, that in 2003, Nucor reconfigured the Memphis facility throughout. The irony, Don said, is that several players in both scenarios were the same due to the combination of companies.

"If it had not been for Birmingham Steel, Nucor would not be here today," Don affirmed. "We were able to get the road access, open the park and put rail in." Nucor is a $300 million capital project on top of Birmingham Steel's original investment. Not only that, but Nucor has put in a high transmission electrical line and has purchased 120 additional acres on its north side.

The Super Terminal project opened in 2005 – the same year Brian left the public sector. It has taken many twists and turns along the way. That was 10 years after Brian entered the office and 10 years after Uniport first conducted a small study on container rail traffic in Memphis. Now called Gateway Memphis, it was known in planning circles as the Memphis Joint Inter-modal Terminal Project. What also fed into this in the background is Illinois Central being purchased by CN in 2002.

The city started dealing with IC at first. When IC was bought by Canadian National things moved much more aggressively in local development circles. "CN got serious about working with us and contracted for 250 acres," Randy Richardson said. Construction began immediately and opened in 2005 when two subsequent expansions hit in 2007 and 2008.

CHANGING TIMES LEADS TO ANOTHER RETIREMENT

Brian's role played an important step in helping make long-run uses for the industrial park a reality with his coordinating position on behalf of city and county planning. But after almost 10 years in the public sector, Brian saw first-hand how arduous it was to get things done. One could even say that high hurdles became the pervasive order of the week. Unlike working in the private sector, politics became more prevalent in getting good business done in an unexpected completion time.

"I began to lack more and more ownership of the events taking place and events became too legalistic," he recalled. "I was used to the private sector and prided myself in creativity, flexibility and quick action." He quickly realized that he could no longer continue to put up with such challenges. "I just could not get as much accomplished." At the end of 2004, he wrote his retirement letter to both Shelby County Mayor Wharton and Memphis Mayor Herenton.

"My decision to retire from public life was driven by the politics of things not getting done fast enough and the measure of ownership I could have of events," he said. "I was used to quick action and meeting deadlines."

Dexter has a supplemental perspective on the overall picture: "Being your own boss as a senior vice president at FedEx – you tell someone to do something and they do it. In the public sector there is hesitation or non-responsiveness. It was a hard transition to make, but he made it. You are under a lot of scrutiny in the public sector with the media. It is also a very political environment with people having different motivations than you have (toward objectives you are trying to reach)."

Today, Brian finds it distressing to see what is happening in Memphis in Shelby County because of government activities or inactivity over the last two decades. This has caused the city and county to fall behind - vis-à-vis other ends of the state – not to mention the progress of other comparative cities.

Dexter recalls about the years they worked together, "He was really passionate about his work. His work and leisure were really not that separate. He rarely took a break from work. What he wanted was to give back to the community and he had a strong sense of duty, duty to family, to church and work. Brian had a lot of respect for people. He didn't think of people who worked for him as subordinates. Everyone was always impressed by the way he treated people. He might have been perceived as dogmatic but he had real convictions about things. He exudes a confidence to deal with issues but can be very demanding. Because he was thorough and methodical, he would not tend to make spot decisions. His preference would be to do the homework every time rather than make a rapid decision."

Before Brian retired from the Memphis/Shelby County position, he was approached by Pat Harcourt of Askew Hargraves Harcourt (A2H) who admired Brian's way of getting things done. They both also shared a love of aviation. Soon, Brian sat down and talked with the other principals, Mark Askew and Ed Hargraves.

True to his method of operation, Brian's retirement was short lived. He joined the A2H efforts as a business consultant to develop future projects because of the people he knew, particularly with the Tennessee Department of Transportation and city and state leaders. He was able to get some entrees for the engineering firm. He also was able to talk with authority to representatives of regional and fixed base operation airports. This translated into potential specialty business for the engineering group. These talks also involved conversations with the Tennessee Industrial Development Council and participants of the Tennessee Governors Conference and Engineers Day on "the Hill." Contacts he previously made with various legislative people, with MLGW and TVA paid off as well. It employs a best practice he advocates of redeploying network contacts attained over the years. "You're able to reuse the equity you build up, the goodwill of a career."

In a vaguely similar vein, he consulted for the Memphis office of New Jersey-based OI Partners (also known as Russell Montgomery & Associates) led by Bob Reilly, the local principal. Bob approached Brian, asking if he'd consider some work for his group that was heavily engaged in outplacement counseling and leadership training for professionals. Unfortunately, it was about the time that his wife, Peg, began to encounter poor health. That prevented Brian from going full throttle with either venture to the extent he otherwise could.

All the same, this chapter in Brian's life shone brightly. In Dexter's words, Brian's accomplishments were strong and lived long. "Economic development is a business about relationships and decisions are often made on intangibles too – not just the numbers," Dexter commented. "Trust is a huge thing and Brian had the trust of prospect businesses and local industry. With him there were no hidden agendas and he didn't play games. Behind his thorough analysis, he cares a lot about Memphis. He balanced duty to family, his work and church."

BRIAN'S LESSONS LEARNED:

1. Think responsibly and consider others when making decisions.

2. When government and the public sector work together the result is good stewardship and public policy.

11

A LIFE OF FAITH
AND SERVICE

Brian's faith, along with his tenacity for seeing
things to completion, is best observed through his
years of prolonged church involvement. He grew up
in a Protestant Episcopalian family in a predominately Catholic area of Berkshire County, Mass. A
majority of his friends were Catholic as well as
his wife Peg. Despite the strong Catholic influence, Brian was true to his Episcopalian beliefs,
which stemmed from the influence of his paternal
grandmother. Brian has often stated that he will
always be a "cradle-to-grave" Episcopalian.

Religion always had an influence on Brian and has had a strong affect on his view of the world. After being first exposed to religion by his parents, his faith has grown and continues to guide and influence him. His longtime friend, Phil Irish, says, "While he is not outwardly and religious in a showy way, he is guided by a very religious sense of treating everyone well and that is a leadership attribute many in business don't seem to have."

Brian always believed, and studies have shown, that people in a religious environment, are more positive, healthier, and have a better view of life than those without those traditional values. Through college, the Air Force, to the corporate and business world, and then city government, Brian's traditional value system helped guide his decisions. However, his spiritual side wasn't always in the forefront of his life or his decision making. He didn't consciously pray about every decision. In his early years he was too busy with work and was not focused on the spiritual aspect nearly to the degree he was later on. His relationship with God became more apparent to him after the age of 35. Now in his 70s, Brian reflects on several factors that contributed to his deepening faith. As the years go by, he thinks more about his father's spiritual journey and how he is making a similar journey now. Additionally, the loss of Peg in 2007 contributed to his deepening spirituality. "When you lose your wife after 48 years, these events can kick you into another gear and take you to another spiritual level," Brian recalled.

THE CHURCH OF THE HOLY APOSTLES

After moving the family to Memphis in 1974 to begin a new career with Federal Express, Brian and Peg began the search for a church that met the needs of their family. Even though Peg was Catholic, Brian's Episcopalian roots went deeper. Therefore, there was little debate about what church they would attend. Around the same time, Harry and Mona Sherrick, a family known by the Pecons who attended the same Episcopal parish in Tulsa, also moved to Memphis. Ironically, both families decided to become members of the same parish in Memphis. Initially located in Hickory Hill, The Church of the Holy Apostles became their new church home. Holy Apostles is a daughter church of Church of the Holy Communion located at Perkins and Walnut Grove in Memphis.

The small Episcopal congregation began with a group of believers in the late 1960s. Meeting first at the Evans Elementary School on Clarke Road, many of the members came from other churches in the Parkway Village community. The Pecons were among one of the first families to join the growing congregation. Only a handful of families that remain with the church today pre-date them. By 1974, a contemporary church building and sanctuary on Knight Arnold Road was completed and consecrated.

These were stressful times for Brian who had just started a new job with a small upstart company known as Federal Express. Having to balance family, work and church, he did not always embrace religion as a daily regimen. "When I was involved with Federal in the early years it consumed me – hook, line and sinker. Your mind and soul are literally absorbed daily with your work efforts." Additionally, he and Peg were heavily involved with golf and community activities on the side. The church and golf provided stability and countered some of the stress that runs high in the corporate world. According to Brian, faith and church were important and stabilizing influences.

Brian became involved in the financial aspects of his church shortly after he and his family began attending Holy Apostles. Serving on the Finance and Capital Campaign Committees, he encountered one of his first challenges. It was apparent that many people provided donations to build the church, but there were many IOUs. The intent of the donor was to give a certain amount to the new church facility and pay down the mortgage over the next few years. However, there were several large pledges that were not paid according to their commitment. With fresh debt on the newly dedicated building, he and the financial team of the church were able to solve the issue by starting their own capital campaign to raise the necessary capital.

According to the Diocese, small churches like Holy Apostles started out as mission churches. By the mid-80s they were able to climb out of the mission status and become a full-fledged parish. By the late 1980s the church grew to over 400 communicants. The Pecons and other dedicated members were heavily involved in the growth process, adeptly and properly leveraging the financial strength of the church.

Holy Apostles experienced many changes during the early 1980s and into the 1990s. The need for expansion spurred a new church sanctuary, which was completed and consecrated in 1987. Additionally, the church had several changes in priests over the years, causing some parishioners to decide to "visit other churches." As a result, Holy Apostles became a transient parish in the mid-80s. Priests moved through the parish to and from various assignments. Usually, they left for external reasons, but in one instance, the Bishop initiated the change.

A SIGN OF THE TIMES

In 1990, the first female priest was assigned to the church. This was a big step for Holy Apostles because no female had ever served as a principal priest in the West Tennessee Dioceses. Brian served with five others on the selection committee, which was comprised of both male and female members. The selection committee conducted interviews and made its recommendation to the 12-member Vestry, who ultimately made the final selection. A consultation from the Bishop was also a necessary step in the process. From a field of one female and three male candidates, Anne Carriere was selected as the first female rector of the parish. Brian supported her selection because he believed she was the best candidate for the post. Some female parish members were against the choice, especially the older women in the Parish. However, most of the males were neutral. A few members left the church because of the decision, but not a significant number. Many of the younger and middle aged females thought it was a good choice. Ann Carriere served as Priest of the Church of the Holy Apostles until February, 1997.

Brian's business and financial background made him a great asset to the church. In the 1990s, he started to develop a much stronger dedication to his church. He served as a Senior Warden and Vestry member several times. Peg was also very active and served as both Junior and Senior Warden. With his business background, it is no surprise that Brian became involved with almost every financial decision made by the church from the late 1970s to the present day. Financing tends to be one of the most challenging aspects in church management, but Brian's knowledge and guidance helped the church successfully meet a variety of challenges for over 30 years.

He was elected to the Diocesan Standing Committee and also served as Chair of the Diocesan Finance Committee. He was also elected as an alternate to the National Convention twice and served on the Diocese's Bishop and Council, which is the Vestry for Episcopalian dioceses. Made up of lay and clergy members, the Standing Committee serves when there is no Bishop in the Diocese and also interviews and recommends prospective candidates for the priesthood.

RELOCATION — A DIFFICULT DECISION

A pivotal event for the church occurred in 2000. Due to the changing demographics of the black and white communities, the area surrounding the predominately white church was rapidly becoming a black neighborhood. At the same time, John Urban, a temporary priest assigned by the Bishop, approached Brian with the news that a local developer representing the Walgreen Company was interested in purchasing the church property at the intersection of Hickory Hill and Knight Arnold roads. This interest set into motion a series of crucial steps for the church, which was losing members almost weekly to newer residential developments in Collierville, Germantown and north Mississippi. The question was apparent – should the church stay and embrace the changing community or relocate? The original offer to sell the property to Walgreens, the largest drug store chain in the U.S. was at first rejected by the church leaders, but soon a second offer was made. Brian and the leadership of the church struggled for the right answer. Could the Holy Apostles Church survive at their original location? The question of relocating church membership was met with mixed emotions by the communicants and many members became split on the issue. Brian, along with several other

THE
LIVING CHURCH

PARISH ADMINISTRATION ISSUE

AN INDEPENDENT WEEKLY SERVING EPISCOPALIANS • SEPTEMBER 10, 2006 • $2.50

Church of the Holy Apostles, Collierville, Tennessee

Church of the Holy Apostles construction (L to R) Brian Pecon, Bob
Capra, Reverend Jenny Cooper, Carey Mayfield, George Kawell, Alice
Finn, and Reverend Barkley Thompson, Collierville, TN, 2006.

Interior of Church of the Holy Apostles, Collierville, TN.

church leaders believed the church could no longer grow in its current location. This was not the first time they faced difficult church issues.

Another issue that complicated the decision was that of race. An African-American start-up congregation was using the facility on a part-time basis. Some members thought they could be absorbed with the Holy Apostles base congregation, but this became a very heated issue among the parishioners for many months. Attendance began to drop and no solution to reestablishing the growth of the church could be found. After a prayerful process by the church leaders, a recommendation was made to sell the church property, a decision supported by the Diocese.

The 8.5-acre property was sold in August 2001 and a Walgreens store was ultimately built on the property. A search for a new church home was initiated immediately. The sale of this property allowed Holy Apostles to pay off all of its diocesan debts and to eventually purchase a new site. Interestingly, the Diocese allowed the Parish to keep the money from the sale to purchase property and to build a new facility. For the next two years, the search for a new church home was the focus for the church leaders. Brian recalls the fortunate event, "We were the divine beneficiary of being able to sell the property and get the support of the Diocese to boot." The original 1974 sanctuary remains today and is now occupied by the Memphis Alzheimer's Association.

The search for a new church location began in 2001 and continued through 2003. During this time Holy Apostles met in the Faith Presbyterian Church at Shelby Drive and Germantown Road under the leadership of Reverend Bill Kelly, the Diocesan-appointed vicar.

In June of 2003, the Bishop assigned a curate, Barkley Thompson, to lead Holy Apostles at Agape Chapel at St. George's Independent School. He was outgoing, personable, and well educated and many felt he was perfect for the new congregation. The new curate, with the help of Brian and the church leaders, elevated the church from mission to parish status. This enabled Holy Apostles to initiate a new capital campaign; find a new site and begin the planning and design work for the new building. Although several alternate locations were considered, this new high-growth area seemed to be the logical spot. Their primary focus was to find a location where the church could grow and prosper. In the fall of 2005 ground was broken and construction began on the 8-acre location on Wolf River Blvd. in Collierville. Brian and Bob Capra served as Building Committee co-chairs during Phase I of the construction. Later, Brian chaired Phase II for a Parish Life Center addition to accommodate a growing space requirement for youth and adult Christian educational needs. Brian also served as co-chair with Alice Finn on the new Capital Campaign Committee. From the sale of the old property, the church was able to purchase a 120-acre site near the Wolf River bottoms. Interestingly, all but 13.5 acres used for the church campus was resold to The Chickasaw Basin Authority, a public, non-profit agency. The funds from the sale of this surplus acreage allowed the parish to reduce the land purchase debt over 25 percent. Currently, the church is very active and thriving, with about 450 members.

A TRIBUTE TO BRIAN'S WORK

The current rector, John Leach, recently established an annual award in Brian's name, the Brian Pecon Lay Ministry Award. An award of this type, normally awarded posthumously, is in recognition for his devotion and commitment as well as service to the church, and is quite an honor for it to be bestowed upon someone still living. "When we presented him with the honor in his name at the church, he didn't know it ahead of time and was genuinely moved," said Father Leach of Holy Apostles. "It celebrates his sense of determination and faithfulness. He is one who rarely makes a decision without being well informed and sees a project through without letting up. He is dogged about it and expects the same energy from others. He's very methodical and analytic and is well informed before he acts."

John also noted that Brian is genuinely a servant leader. "He is motivated by the good leadership he sees in others. He has a vested interest in making people successful. And it is good to have someone with creative problem-solving skills in our church because he does not shy away from problems. Brian sees faith as a responsibility to do everything and be everything he can be."

Despite his commitment to Holy Apostles, Brian recently decided to step down as the Chairman of the Finance Committee after more than 30 years of service to the church. Brian reflects, "I feel good and sleep at night based on my faith and spirituality. I've been able to assist in the successful completion of a 19,000-square-foot facility with assets of over $4 million. I am satisfied that the current Finance Committee is exceptionally well-qualified to provide fiscal leadership for Holy Apostles' growth."

Realizing that he met these projects with the same intensity as other business pursuits, Brian remains humble regarding his role. "Some people may make glowing statements about how they were struck from above or it was a message from God to do the work they did with the church, but with me it was not that way at all." It was all very natural for Brian as he began to realize that everything happens for a reason.

He always set a good example of religious faith and service for his family, but never tried to force them into a rigid set of religious beliefs or to be members of the Episcopal Church. Brian and Peg always allowed their daughters to go their own way and choose their own spiritual direction.

Brian's faith coupled with a "can do attitude" led him to pick up a spiritual cause. As his sense of spirituality deepened, he felt compelled to use his management and leadership skills to help the church. It was his tenacity and drive that placed him in a position to help grow a struggling parish of 35 to a successful new church of over 350 communicants. His "can do attitude" is obvious and his family considers his work with the church to be among his greatest accomplishments in life.

His story is one of emergence, struggling with challenges, surmounting them, experiencing some setbacks, surviving, succeeding and moving onward. Nevertheless, Brian himself realizes it was not his own doing.

"Over the years, it struck me how neatly events have fallen into place – certainly more than I could have planned. I give credit to the Lord's work. How does all this factor into reinventing yourself? Without faith, you don't have the steadiness and calmness to go along with the stubborn perseverance."

BRIAN'S LESSONS LEARNED:

1. Decisions are often guided by intuition. Focus on your goals, and be in touch with your inner self and your sense of community.

2. Fight for what you believe in; stay the course and keep your faith strong for you to persevere.

12

---✦---

"HALF A CENTURY AT WORK – SIGNIFICANCE FOR TODAY AND TOMORROW"

Brian's passion for the first 30 to 40 years of his life primarily consisted of aviation and the thirst for adventure. This is obvious with his love for flying and his interest in the airline industry. Later in life, Brian found his entrepreneurial side and realized he had a passion for life and all of its challenges. Meeting each of these challenges became his driving force and fueled his need to succeed.

Brian is a man who could have retired early long ago. Instead, he kept investing in his community and, chiefly, in his church. Through and through, his definition of success lies neither in monetary accumulation, nor the balance sheets, rather, to the degree a man can ply his talents into his world. It all is wrapped up in his overall work ethic. Working six days a week is not overworking, in his mind. "If I don't have multiple things going on, I'm bored," he humbly said. "Then I feel I have too much time on my hands. I have always thought that way."

His motivation was not fame or fortune. He set out to do well in his work and to raise a family, while contributing to his community along the way. He went from the Air Force to graduate school to American Airlines, FedEx, Specialty Lube, M&P Associates, the public sector and then consulting with few extended breaks. Stopping to rest never occurred to him. This is a man with a built-in work ethic. "I didn't feel the need to go off for a month's sabbatical," he said. "I didn't need to separate myself from other events going on.

I had a few brief respites, but overall, it just seems life is like a continuum." While he may not have been a true entrepreneur, he was very innovative with the tools he was given or the ones he acquired. He didn't allow a fear of failure to influence his decision-making, to be sure. Measured risk-taking was almost the norm for him. He took a risk when turning down the Air Force Regular commission without full knowledge that his family business was being sold. He ventured into Russia to try and develop a cancer hospital. He was willing to take major leaps when they made sense to him after analyzing many business angles. With Brian, one important attribute separates him from the average business man: his belief in doing your homework first.

Brian developed a knack for seeing many sides of an argument or negotiation and had the ability to engender trust. He did this by being a servant-leader. He would practice what he preached by actually doing what he would tell others to do. That involves forging realistic plans, having stretch goals and action plans for execution, true transferable concepts for others. Brian would review situations, plan and synchronize those plans with other team members. Persistence also played a major part in the way he dealt with challenges. "I sometimes see people at business meetings putting on a façade. From experience, I can tell those who are genuine and those who are not. At least when people meet me and know me, what you see is what you are getting."

Corporate executives often glean valuable lessons and insights from others in terms of transferable strategies of big picture-thinking and innovation. What you see in them is their vision. They fill niches in their industries and expand those niches. Brian enjoyed a sense of building things and seeing new vistas. He was a risk-taker, but quantified strategies objectively and financially. Behind all that was the value of building a team of qualified people who knew how to get the job done.

Something that concerns Brian today is the loss of the business "work ethic" in the younger generations. "Today it is quite different from generations past. One difference is the lack of loyalty to a company. If this continues, we may experience some leadership issues down the road." Truly, future workers and employees will be living to work more than working to live as was the case in previous generations. Therefore, it will be important going forward that a real sense of earned loyalty will need to become a two-way street between employers and employees.

It is a generally accepted notion that over the last few years, only 17 percent of workers consider themselves "happy" with their jobs, thus the balance of that percentage would be in the non-content category. Employers could emphasize more non-salary benefits in terms of flex time, specialized skills training, membership in wholesale buying clubs, company retreats, worker performance incentive trips and other inventive practices.

"This phenomenon obviously sets a stage for the need to refine their ability to uniquely contribute in whatever market area or industry they chose to select," Brian notes.

"Change is coming faster, which further accelerates each succeeding generation's need to continuously reinvent themselves in our predominantly U.S. service economy, which is no longer an industrial economy. In all likelihood, I can see a trend where older employees will not leave the workforce as quickly and will stay active in the workforce until their 70s. Perhaps it is time to increase the time-honored retirement age of 65 to a level somewhat higher as healthcare improves."

Clearly, Brian's work life never was just a job. That is why it continues to this day. "You excel in things you have a drive and a passion for." His desire to leave this legacy is part of his rationale. It is part of his purpose in life – his justification for completing a task; it's the way he is wired.

Looking back, perhaps Brian – as most of us would – wishes he had known some of the lessons learned sooner. Simply knowing how to go from here to there is fundamental but important. Knowing how to change when you hit stumbling blocks along the way is essential. He learned through experience to stop, analyze, modify and continue on the journey, always being persistent. Brian reflected on one important life lesson, "As I get older, I'm beginning to see that having a true sense of vision is more important than getting lost in the details."

When asked if he regretted any of his decisions, Brian quickly answered with an unqualified "No." Although, he did reflect, "If I had it to do again, I would spend more time with the family, because it is obvious I didn't spend a lot of time with them. People who cannot reconcile their personal and professional lives and choose career over family usually wind up with bigger family related problems. Hopefully, time spent with my grandchildren will provide some restitution. My bank account isn't as great as some, but my personal baggage load is pretty damn low. That lack of baggage is an important factor in living a good life, but in the long run, the most important element is the family."

Like others, there are a number of times in his life when he thought the world had thrown him a mountain to climb, but his can-do attitude and perseverance continued to drive his need to succeed. "I'm not a particularly smart guy. My road through flight training and academics is more due to tenacity and an attitude – by God, if they can do it, I can too. I have had to fight more for things in my life. I now see this trait in my daughters and hopefully in my grandchildren."

Brian always displayed a high degree of self-confidence and determination. Once he put his mind to something, it was "get out of my way." That's being driven. He has had a life of service and wouldn't be happy unless he was busy. Now at age 73, Brian continues to work on projects he feels serve an important purpose to the Memphis/Shelby County community. Among these are:

- Memphis Belle Memorial Association Board
- St. Columbia Episcopal Conference Center Board
- Church of the Holy Apostles
- Germantown Economic Development Commission
- Economic Club of Memphis
- Memphis Alzheimer Day Service Advisory Committee
- Concord Academy Board
- Methodist Germantown Hospital Advisory Board

Brian says it best, "I'm probably driven to stay busy unnecessarily - I mean, my God, I'm just not going to stop until the time comes and I wind up in a hospital or whatever. Maybe the right thing to do for some is to go live in a retirement home. I keep getting calls from one – hey, but I'm not ready for that."

FAMILY PERSPECTIVES

Brian Pecon's family life has experienced an assortment of ups and downs as is the case with most families and is far from perfect. One factor remains prominent: he loves and cherishes his family more with each passing year. Since losing his beloved wife, Peg, in November of 2007, he tends to reflect and focus more on how the family evolved and about his role as provider, husband, and father. Now at age 73, he spends much more time than he used to with his daughters and also much of his time with grandchildren.

Brian shared the fact that the first of the Pecon children came into the world in typical Air Force fashion. Pamela Jean was born in 1960 and Priscilla Ann was born the following year. "We started the family quickly," Brian recalls. "I mean nine and a half months after the wedding we had Pam and seventeen months later, Priscilla arrived. Both Peg and I wondered if we were going a bit too fast." Both Pam and Priscilla were born in the on-base hospital at Davis Monthan Air Force Base in Tucson, Ariz. (with a military co-payment fee of $7.50 and $8 respectively). Moving at a much slower pace in terms of growing their family, their third daughter, Patricia Lynn, was born eight and a half years later in 1970 in Tulsa at a cost of $750.

Air Force family life in the early 1960s was anything but normal. The oldest girls did not recall seeing their father often, which is understandable considering his Strategic Air Command alert status duties and obligations as a military pilot. Thus continued the strict cycle of being driven to every goal he established for himself.

Because of the tremendous workload he constantly carried, it was sometimes difficult for Brian to relate to his children. True of many fathers, it seemed as if he was often too busy and under too much pressure to spend a lot of time with the family. As a result, Brian had very little patience with them in those early years. That has certainly changed today as he's built a stronger and more loving relationship with his daughters, especially his seven grandchildren.

The oldest daughters, Pam and Priscilla, never felt very close to their father until much later in life. During their early years, their father (as his father did) displayed the old school philosophy that children should be "seen and not heard." This is not surprising, considering the traditional upbringing by his parents. To his daughters, Brian was the traditional disciplinarian and often seemed "grumpy" around the house. He appeared to them as being too rigid, too "military" and too structured. His behaviors and attitudes were very much in keeping with his own father. Priscilla recalls, "I'm sure he loved us and was looking out for us, but he always had a bigger picture in his mind." That "bigger picture" estimation also was sometimes observed by his co-workers.

There were times, due to his work, when the girls felt an alienation of affections. For example, according to Pam, "The only time he actually said he was proud of me was when I graduated from college with my bachelor's degree. It floored me because I had never heard him say it before. He was never able to tell me how he felt when I was young, but today, I value his opinion very much. He is very good at looking at things level-headedly. One of the things I admire most about him is that he will not speak negatively about people. I never heard him say an ill word about anybody. He was always very politically correct and diplomatic."

"My father was always serious at home, so he never laughed much," Pam recalls. "Once, when we were small, my parents had a pretty bad argument. Mom told him she was packing up the kids and leaving. My father paused a moment then started laughing. His laughter became uncontrollable and tears began to run down his face. My mother then began to laugh and they stood there and laughed at each other. My sisters and I just stood there and stared at them. That was the first time I ever heard him really laugh."

After reflecting upon his life for the past few years, Brian now sees his daughters in a much different light. He is very proud of all of them and their respective accomplishments. According to Brian, "Pam puts a lot of work into what she does. Deep down, I knew she had the perseverance to do whatever she wanted, but I never gave her a lot of advice. I was not as supportive with my girls as they are now with their own kids. They are much more caring than

(L to R) Brian and Peg's daughters Pamela, Tricia, and Priscilla, 1990.

Parents Fiftieth Wedding Anniversary (L to R) Brian Pecon, Diana Pecon,
Leon Pecon, Janice McNaughton, Bruce Pecon, South Lee, MA, 1983.

I was at their age. I came from the old school, born in 1937, I had a pretty rigid old-style father, and by God, I've kind of followed in that track."

Pam mentions how her father's parents had a great influence on her. Brian always felt there was a strong similarity between him and his father. However, his mother probably had a stronger influence than his father in regard to religion, matters of faith and being more organized and administratively driven toward financial matters.

Both Pam and Priscilla are strong-willed people, learning much from their parents. Priscilla recalled her father was a very driven man – a man with a purpose. "I didn't have a close relationship with him when I was growing up because he was always working on his plan to have an engineering degree – to have an MBA – to have this job or that job – to be successful. He always had his eyes set on the direction he wanted to take in life." Because he was so driven to succeed, he would sometimes put family second. According to both Pam and Priscilla, "He had high expectations for us and urged us to shoot for the top of everything, but his priorities in the early years were job first – wife second – then the kids."

Family Gathering (L to R) First Row — Addison Forsdick, Jenny McKenzie, Madeline Forsdick, Tricia Forsdick, Pamela McKenzie, Mae Forsdick, Peg Pecon, Priscilla Svoboda, April Svoboda. Second Row — Ryan McKenzie, Andrew Forsdick, John McKenzie, Brian Pecon, Chip Svoboda, Reece McKenzie, Destin, FL, 2007.

Pam shared one important note of character, "I never had the impression growing up that his main objective was money. My sole impression was that his goal was simply to succeed in whatever he tackled. He is very results oriented and always has a project going on."

None of the daughters remembers confiding in their father in those early years and rarely saw him openly display affection. What they did see was a man driven by himself and the high stress of demanding jobs, trying very hard to provide a good living for his family. In spite of their father's toughness, he set for them a high work ethic. This example helped make them stronger and more self reliant through the years. "It was a plus for me. If someone tries to bully me around now – it isn't going to happen," Priscilla remarked. Fortunately, time has changed any harsh feelings they may have had for their father from those early years. Recently, they have all grown much closer together as a family.

Patricia (Trish), who was considered "the baby," had a slightly different perception of her father. She remembers him as a "passionate and stubborn, but fair man." Being the youngest, Trish's early memories of her father are understandably vague but she remembers often sitting in his study with him as he worked. He would sometimes read to her. "There was one chair in particular he always sat in. I would wait for him to read to me in that chair. It was a good memory," she recalled. To Trish, her father always seemed a little "harder" on her two sisters than on her, probably because they were older. Interestingly she reflected, "I want my kids to be more like he is now than he was in the early years. He seems more human now that he is older."

Brian considers himself blessed when he thinks of his three daughters, each accomplished in her own right. Impressed by the fact that all three prospective sons-in-law asked Brian for permission to marry, he feels very fortunate to have three who are good fathers and husbands. "I wonder if my father had grown up in these times, if he would have been the same," Brian reflects. "I look at my sons-in-law today and they are quite good fathers. They display love and affection and direction with their kids, much more than my father or I ever did. I guess this is simply a sign of the times."

Brian's younger brother, Bruce, revealed several attributes that reflect Brian's strong management and leadership skills. "He is strongly committed to whatever task he starts. He tends to be stubborn, yet has learned to be empathetic and compromising through the years. Brian is likeable and has made many friends. His ability as a leader and a manager has made him a man that gets things done. This is actually a quality instilled by our parents. He is also a deeply religious man, strong in his faith and beliefs."

Due to his busy schedule, Brian rarely took a vacation, but when he did the family trips usually consisted of short jaunts to visit parents and family in Massachusetts and Florida. In keeping with his method of operation, these trips were usually scheduled and organized events, carried out with some degree of precision. Impromptu getaways for him were unlikely. However, Peg would often take the girls to visit family without Brian, when he had commitments.

Brian described himself and Peg as opposites, however, in many ways Peg was the perfect wife for Brian. Mary Irish, one of Peg's best friends commented, "They were like two peas in a pod. Peg was a quiet person until she knew you better – then she could be very direct and straightforward. She had a strong persona and was always in control. Once she had a large party at her home and waited two days before beginning any preparations. Undaunted by her lack of planning, the gathering was a huge success." She was a passionate, fiery Scots-Irish redhead and could always match Brian's wit and temperament.

Brian with seven grandkids plus one (Julianne Cordera), 2009.

They had a very strong bond. Both said exactly what they thought and she was rarely intimidated by him. Peg was known for her dry wit and could be very spontaneous. Her biggest love outside of her home and family was the game of golf, which she continued to play until health problems plagued her later in life. She could often be found playing at Ridgeway and Southwind, two of her favorite courses. Although she spent countless hours playing the game, she helped organize many of the St. Jude Golf Tournaments. Her support and volunteer work for the St. Jude tournament has not gone unnoticed. Brian recalled, "Without her help and support, the girls never would have turned out as well, nor would we have survived without her working in Boston, Rochester or Tulsa. That family togetherness was created by her own stability and tenacity."

In March 1998 Peg was initially diagnosed with lung cancer after passing out on the kitchen floor in their Germantown home. The diagnoses revealed two types of blockage; carotid artery blockage (90 percent on one side and 95 percent on the other) and heart blockage which required triple bypass heart surgery to correct the heart issues. Her X-rays also showed a non-metastasized lung cancer in the left lower lobe which was removed about three months after the heart problem was stabilized. Her overall health seemed relatively fine until early 2007 when she began to complain of back problems. She took a fall in the new church kitchen and dislocated her right shoulder in April 2007. Back pains became increasingly worse from the multiple myloma (a form of cancer). She finally realized her days of playing golf, a sport she had loved and played for years, had ended.

In late September of 2007, Peg visited an oncologist who wanted to administer an experimental drug. However, her daughter Pam thought the drug was too dangerous and the family collectively decided against this move. She spent five weeks in the Germantown Methodist Hospital and had one week of therapy in the Methodist University hospital downtown. Unfortunately, she never regained her strength. The earlier lung cancer had quickly advanced and with the simultaneous multiple myloma her condition became difficult to treat. The doctors elected not to give her chemotherapy and informed the family that she would probably not recover. Peg died on November 9, 2007.

The public support displayed at the Memorial Park wake and at the Church of the Holy Apostles funeral was a fitting tribute to her caring life. She was interred at the new church Columbarium. Contributions to her memory are displayed in the Holy Apostles Church patio and garden arrangements.

Brian contends that he was not always the most caring and loving man with his family. There was never a lot of sentimentality and emotion displayed between Brian and Peg. They rarely displayed their affection outwardly in the 48 and one-half years of marriage. Brian recalls, "There was no need. We thought there would always be a tomorrow to show affection. She had in her mind when she was sick to just get up after a while and go play golf – or go to Tunica with her traveling Bunco girls' group of 25 years. That was just her way – to be direct and strong. I think that attribute carried over to our daughters' ability to stand on their own two feet." Brian added, "Life will just not be the same for us, but we all feel blessed for all the time and memories we had together, especially with every grandchild that Peg lived to see."